The 1984
Price Guide
to Goss China

WILLIAM HENRY GOSS

The inventor of heraldic porcelain. This view was used as a New Year card by W.H. in 1885 when he was aged 52

ADOLPHUS WILLIAM HENRY GOSS

The eldest son of W.H., he joined the firm in the 1880's and was responsible for the introduction of heraldic china

VICTOR HENRY GOSS

The third son of W.H., he ran the factory from 1906 until his tragic death in 1913

WILLIAM HUNTLEY GOSS

The youngest son of W.H., he unwillingly joined the firm in the late 1890's and was left in sole charge from 1913 until he sold the business in 1928

237756

£4

£1

David Singmaster
9 May 2004

38 ✓
40 ✓
224 ?
227 ?

The 1984
Price Guide
to Goss China

Nicholas Pine

Milestone Publications

© Nicholas Pine 1984

All rights reserved. No part of this publication may be reproduced, stored in a retrieval system, or transmitted in any form, or by any means, whether electronic, mechanical, photocopying, recording or otherwise, without the prior permission of Milestone Publications except for brief passages in criticism or review.

Published by
Milestone Publications
Goss & Crested China Ltd.,
62 Murray Road,
Horndean, Hampshire PO8 9JL

ISBN 0 903852 41 1

Design Brian Iles
Photography Michael Edwards Studio, Havant

Typeset by Inforum Ltd., Portsmouth
Printed and bound in Great Britain by
R. J. Acford, Industrial Estate, Chichester, Sussex

British Library Cataloguing in Publication Data

Pine, Nicholas J.
    The 1984 price guide to Goss china.
    1. Goss porcelain—Prices
    I. Title
    338.4'3738'27   NK4399.G/

    ISBN 0–903852–41–1

Contents

Acknowledgements 6

Introduction 8

W.H. Goss and Goss China 11

Marks on W.H. Goss China 20

Notes for the Collector 25
Minor variations in size 25
Clay Pipes, Teeth and Buttons 25
Forgeries 27
The Blackpool Coat of Arms 27
Registration Numbers 28

Named Models and Special Shapes 30

Cottages, Houses, Churches, etc. 117

Crosses 128

Fonts 131

Animals 135

Domestic and Ornamental Ware 140
A. Table Ware 141
B. Useful Articles 155
C. Ornamental Articles 160
D. Loving Cups and Mugs 172

Metalware 175

Parian Ware 176
A. Busts 176
B. Figures and Groups 190
Ornamental Early Ware 198

Goss England and Late Ware 212
A. Buildings and Monuments 213
B. Flower Girls 217
C. Toby Jugs 222
D. Figures and Animals 223
E. Late Ware carrying the 'W.H. Goss and Gosshawk' and 'W.H. Goss England' trademarks 228
F. Ware marked 'W.H. Goss Cottage Pottery' or 'Royal Buff' 232
G. Hand Painted Ware 235

Miniatures 236

Terra-Cotta 239

Advertising Ware 242

Dolls 243

Postcards 245

Goss Cabinets 246

The Goss Records 248

The League of Goss Collectors 250

Acknowledgements

Once again, the author and publishers wish to thank all those who have notified us of new pieces in order that this catalogue may be updated: in particular S.J. Copeland, Raymond Fine, Jack Gatenby, Joan Green, Len Harris, J. Meikle, Tony Munday, Derrick Lintin, Edward Stansmore, Elizabeth Topham, Peter Tranter and Peter Wrightson. Without exception these collectors have kindly provided photographs of their pieces when requested, thereby affording everyone the benefit of this new information.

Maurice Regnard, David Hazle and Robin, Philip and Simon Riley have all been extremely helpful, as usual, as has a certain Midlands gentleman who wishes to remain anonymous.

Ever available and always willing to assist, John Galpin has helped in so many diverse ways. Without his knowledge and advice this book would have many inaccuracies. Many of the illustrations are of pieces in his collection and to him the author owes a deep debt of gratitude.

We thank Douglas Goodlad and the Leicester Mercury for kindly allowing us to use their superb photographs taken at the Goss factory in Stoke-on-Trent.

Finally, this book would probably never have appeared at all were it not for John D. Magee, who wrote the first price guide published by Milestone and set Goss china on its present popular course. His initial research and energy fired many collectors with the enthusiasm that they still have and if it were not for him many of us would never have started collecting at all.

WILLIAM H. GOSS

Manufacturer of the Original

HERALDIC IVORY PORCELAIN,

STOKE-ON-TRENT, England.

" R. WILLIAM H. GOSS, Stoke-on-Trent, is the well-known manufacturer of original heraldic ivory porcelain. I had the pleasure of a short interview with Mr. Goss, who was able to say, what few other potters could say just then, that his work people were all busy. But then, he is a manufacturer of specialities—and artistic ones at that. 'Goss's Heraldic China' is known to everyone in the trade, and to thousands who have no connection with it. There is probably no other description of ceramics of which there are so many systematic collectors. This is easily explained. All his productions are suitable for presents: they are all artistic and are easily portable, so that friends—even ladies—can carry to the recipients the pleasing mementos they wish them to accept. There are many occasions—birthdays, wedding days, Christmas, and the New Year—on which most of us like to present our intimate friends with some appropriate souvenir. Goss has been something like a national benefactor in providing a number of acceptable, artistic, and not too expensive presents for all these occasions. When a lady has had a few pieces of 'Goss' presented to her, she wishes for more, and buys an attractive piece now and then to add to her store. She is proud to show her possessions to her friends, and when, in turn, they wish to make her a present, they say, 'We will give her a pretty piece of Goss'. That is how 'collectors' are made. I know a lady who never visits a place of interest for the first time without inquiring from local dealers for a piece of 'Goss' china, with the arms of the city, county borough, or town, enamelled in colours upon it. She has a wonderful collection, and as it is known I am connected with the china trade, I fancy it is expected that whenever I visit her I shall take her a new shape in 'Goss' china. Those of us who cannot afford to make a collection of 'Old Wedgwood,' 'Old Bow,' 'Chelsea,' or 'Derby,' can gratify our hobby for artistic china by securing a great variety of Mr. Goss's beautiful ware. The business was founded more than half a century ago by the father of the present proprietor, and the popularity of the ware has increased year by year. Foreign makers were quick to appreciate the saleable value of miniatures as souvenirs, but though they have imitated the style, they cannot supply the beautiful body of the ivory-like porcelain made in such perfection by Mr. Goss. His great forte is in china miniatures in classical and quaint forms, with coats of arms in correct heraldic colours; but he also supplies figures and landscapes with floral and conventional accessories of great artistic merit. I do not know of a city, borough, county or university that is not represented on Goss china. He selects his forms from classical, historical, and artistic sources generally, and amongst his quaint pieces are many representations of the antique. It is impossible to do full justice to this beautiful ware by reproductions in mere black and white. The charm of the heraldic devices is in the effective enamelling in colours."

An extract from THE POTTERY GAZETTE, May 1st 1912

Introduction

This third edition of **The Price Guide to Goss China** contains details of more than fifty new pieces which have come to light since publication of the 1981 guide.

Numerous detail corrections and improvements have been made and the height or other main dimension of virtually every piece has now been given.

The Domestic and Ornamental Wares chapter has been revised and clarified, as have the Goss England and Miniatures chapters.

An additional 400 illustrations will be found in this edition, including, for the first time, those of every known model. Many new Goss England and domestic and ornamental illustrations have been added, reinforcing the guide's position as the standard work on Goss china.

Many pieces listed refer to the Eighth and War Editions of The Goss Record, which were published originally in 1914 and 1916 respectively. They have both been reprinted by Milestone and give the flavour of Goss collecting at the time as well as having a full description of the history and origin of most of the originals from which the Goss models were made.

Prices quoted in this guide are for perfect items only. Worn gilding, faded coats-of-arms, chips, cracks and bad firing flaws will all affect prices substantially. For example, a cottage normally selling at £80.00 could be worth only £30.00 with a chip or £20.00 with a missing chimney. Restoration is probably worthwhile from the appearance viewpoint, but it would not substantially add to the value of a damaged item. Having said that, sub-standard pieces are very popular at present and have risen in value proportionately more than perfect items during recent years.

The reader is reminded that prices given in this guide are for pieces only – not the arms or decorations which they might carry. The one exception to this is matching arms where in the Named Models and Special Shapes Chapter and occasionally elsewhere the additional premium for correct arms is given. For all other decorations please refer to this book's sister volume *Goss China, Arms Decorations and Their Values* by Nicholas Pine which was revised in 1982 and lists and values some 7000 different decorations which may be found on Goss china.

Thus to find the value of any given piece, firstly look it up in the Price Guide, then add any plussage for the decoration given in *Goss China Arms, Decorations and Their Values*.

For information on Crested China other than Goss, please refer to *Crested China* or *The Price Guide to Crested China*, details of which will be found on page 252.

There are two clubs for collectors of Goss china. The Goss Collectors Club (Secretary Mrs. M. Latham, 3 Carr Hall Gardens, Barrowford, Nelson, Lancashire. BB9 6PU) which produces a monthly magazine and holds regular meetings throughout the country and The Crested Circle (Frank Owen, 26 Urswick Road, Dagenham, Essex. RM9 6EA) which publishes a bi-monthly magazine and runs very successful crested china fairs.

The leading forum for buying and selling is 'Goss & Crested China', a 26-page illustrated monthly catalogue published by Goss and Crested China Ltd. Each edition contains hundreds of pieces for sale from our extensive stocks, including examples from all themes and manufacturers.

Prices in this guide are drawn from over fifteen years' experience of buying and selling Goss china, and for the majority of that period making an orderly market in this ware. Auctions have never been a good source of price information as such outlets tend to be used as a clearing house for substandard and inferior wares due to the low prices pertaining and the small attendances of collectors. Such is the specialist nature of the market.

Over the past few years the Goss market has remained remarkably stable with the majority of prices moving only marginally. Prices for cheaper items have firmed whilst less popular pieces over, say £100, have tended to ease, reflecting, perhaps, the tightness of money rather than any surplus of supply over demand. Matching crest values have moved ahead strongly and cottage prices remain firm.

Bearing in mind the virtual collapse of the stamp market and the sharp decline in the value of coins and other similar collectables, the Goss market has shown amazing resilience during the current recession. The reason for this must surely lie in the almost total lack of investor interest in the market. Most pieces are added to collections by collectors and there they stay, only coming onto the market for specific reasons, usually sad ones. There are now few investors who purchase with a view to making a quick profit, and, such is the perversity of life, that collectors who acquire pieces because they like them, usually make a profit when their collections are finally disposed of – without that being the aim at all when the collection was formed.

Value Added Tax has always been a problem in that it is included as part of the normal retail selling price by Goss & Crested China Ltd., but not apparently by many other dealers. Indeed, it has often been found that minor un-registered dealers have been charging the same prices as this Company and in so doing have in effect been charging more than us!

In order therefore that prices in this guide should be directly comparable with those quoted elsewhere, VAT has not been included in the values of items under 100 years old which attract this tax. At the time of writing, VAT is 15% and this amount should be added when directly comparing prices in this guide with those in the 1981 edition, with the exception of early wares such as busts, figures and terracotta which are quoted nett of tax as they are over 100 years old. So please do not think the majority of pieces have gone down in price over the last few years for they have not, but from now onwards they will be quoted in all our price guides nett of Value Added Tax.

Should you wish to sell, you may wish to note that the prices in this guide are used as a basis for purchasing and that we will pay up to, and often above, half the listed price for all items offered. We are the leading buyers and always offer a fair price for every item.

The heading of a special circular issued by the Goss China Company Ltd. to all the former agents stocking Goss china in 1934, announcing the creation of the new firm.

W. H. Goss and Goss China

A century ago collecting Goss china was fast becoming a national hobby. Tiny ivory coloured porcelain shapes decorated with heraldic devices were being sold in fancy stores, libraries, bazaars and souvenir shops countrywide. Unlike the souvenirs of today, these Victorian mementoes were beautifully and carefully made, requiring skill and hand painting. The quality was superb, and the materials used second to none. Underneath each shape was the factory mark W.H. Goss. These souvenirs were not mass produced, nor were they churned out without care or thought. Each piece, as it left each respective stage in its manufacture, was checked for perfection. Any flaw or fault in its moulding, glaze, application of transfer or device, firing or colouring of the coat-of-arms meant its assignment to the tip. The firm's owner, William Henry Goss, had very high standards. He was not as concerned about making a profit as most pot bank owners were, but in keeping his reputation as a manufacturer of top quality porcelain. He had a firm grip on his firm's affairs and products, and had organised strict rules which had to be adhered to, but although he was stern and formidable, he was also capable of much love and compassion, especially to the poor and to those who worked for him. His employees looked upon him as a father and a figurehead. William Henry Goss and his sons were entirely responsible for the Goss products that we collect today.

Research is currently being undertaken to find out more about the Goss family and the factory, and Milestone hopes to publish the resultant book in 1984.

William Henry Goss opened his first factory at the age of 25 in John Street, Stoke-on-Trent in 1858. He housed his young family then comprising his wife, Georgiana who was then 29, and his children Adolphus 5, Georgiana 3 and Godfrey just 1 year old, in Ashfield Cottage, which he leased. The address was simply Ashfield Cottage, Stoke, and it was set in unspoilt woodland.

With his family to support, he set about building up a business manufacturing enamels and parian ware of the highest quality. He went into partnership with a local roofing-tile manufacturer called Mr. Peake who introduced him to the local clay which was a distinctive shade of reddish brown.

This terracotta clay had been mined for centuries there in the pot bank country and was popular and traditional locally. The partnership with Peake was short-lived and William carried on in the same premises in sole charge. He continued to manufacture some terracotta tobacco jars and wine vases, decorated with transfers of Egyptian influence, or cartoons, some of which were his own designs. It was, however, parian ware which provided his main interest.

The Goss factory in Sturgess Street Stoke-on-Trent. The ovens are in the background. Note the Gosshawk carved in stone and set in the gable wall of the factory.

A close up view of the Gosshawk, which is 3' high and 5' across.

His factory premises were situated next to the Cock Inn, and known as the Cock Works. It was also adjacent to the Spode works, run by the Copeland family, his former employers. William had worked there as chief designer in 1857, and prior to that had lived in London, studying art at the London School of Design, then at Somerset House. It was in London that he met many important friends and contacts in the art world, some of which were to prove to be long lasting and to influence his career. He found London was the place to be for educating himself and extending the mind, and decided to meet similar students who also had a thirst for knowledge. He formed a circle of young intelligent men who regularly met at one another's homes for research and study. He was befriended by the then Lord Mayor of London, Alderman W.F.M. Copeland, a man much older than William. Under his guidance he learnt potting and chemistry to an advanced degree, for Copeland owned the Spode porcelain works in Stoke. He also met Samuel Carter Hall, the editor of the *Art Journal* for many years, and Llewellyn Jewitt, the leading expert in British pottery and porcelain at the time. Jewitt wrote the definitive two-volume *Ceramic Art of Great Britain*, with the assistance of Hall and Goss, in 1878.

Goss spent long hours in the many outhouses and sheds in his garden at Ashfield Cottage, conducting experiments and improving his enamels (which were more profitable than his china) and the parian body from which all his early products were made. He had plenty of experience with parian and wanted to improve it. The fashionable parian or statuary porcelain as it was then known, had been invented by John Mountford, a Spode employee, in 1845 to resemble alabaster. William used a particular type of felspar found in St. Roche in Cornwall, now unavailable, and using his own special recipes he produced a distinctive ivory toned body. During these early days 1858 to 1880 his firm made parian figures, groups and busts, pierced baskets, terracotta ware and his own favourite jewelled vases of which few now exist. He perfected a way of securing the cut glass stones into the vases, having previously made such pieces at the Spode works, but the Goss vases were better. He patented his method in 1872, and received a good report in the next edition of *The Reliquary* of which Llewellyn Jewitt was the Editor. He entered several International Exhibitions at which he displayed his choicest specimens and won many awards including a bronze medal at the 1862 Great International Exhibition. An engraving of the display was originally illustrated in Cassell's illustrated Family Paper and has now been reproduced in John Magee's *Goss for Collectors, The Literature*.

In 1870 William moved his men and plant to the present site in Sturgess Street, Stoke. This street did not then exist and the original address was London Road. The site was the land immediately in front of his Ashfield Cottage home, and he had a path especially constructed so he could walk from one to the other. He usually worked in his factory in the mornings only as he spent his afternoons either going for long walks, working in his sheds or reading and

The Goss bottle ovens as they are today.

writing. He personally organised production and helped in the modelling of the busts which were all of famous people of the time. W.W. Gallimore was his chief designer, and one of the best in the land. This did not deter William's habit of taking over his sculptures when near completion and finishing them off himself! From a model produced by the artist a mould, comprising two or more sections, would be made, and from this further busts were produced. One can often detect the seam line in the manufactured models.

These early Goss products entirely suited the Victorian customers' typically sober, classical style, so popular at the time.

By 1880, very fine tea services were the firm's latest innovation, from a breakfast sized teacup down to a minute miniature, difficult to pick up between finger and thumb. It was in 1883 that Adolphus joined his father in management, and he certainly made some changes. He was a bright, intelligent and confident young man who could see that there was only a limited market for the more expensive figure groups and busts. He could see how life was changing for much of the working class, how improvements in wages and working conditions had made them better off, and that the increasing popularity of trains and paddle steamers had improved transport. There was a growing market for cheap souvenirs especially in seaside holiday resorts. Queen Victoria had made bathing respectable and so during the summer months the resorts were packed with trippers who all wanted to take a present home to their friends, or as a memento of their holiday. By the 1870's his father was making little white glazed vases with the enamelled coats-of-arms of certain public schools and colleges as gifts for those schools' pupils at prize-giving for example. Adolphus thought it viable to apply an assortment of arms on these vases for sale to the general public. William initially rejected Adolphus' ideas but eventually allowed him to experiment. His first designs were ancient armours, seagulls and butterflies. Shapes progressed from pots and vases to models of ancient urns and ewers which were mainly to be found in museums. William himself had a fantastic collection of Roman and Saxon relics and these were housed at home. He had also given Adolphus an old and valuable book on heraldry as a gift, and so he was entirely responsible for his son's ideas. Adolphus soon began producing the coats-of-arms of various towns and resorts, especially those visited by holidaymakers. The popular tourist industry was about to commence.

These heraldic souvenirs met with instant success. There was much work to be done, and working in their small, family way, progress was slower than it might well have been. For immediately, other factories jumped on the band-wagon and imitated the new crested china. But the quality and accuracy of these firms did not match that of the inventor's wares. It was Adolphus himself who was the firm's traveller, appointing retail agents all over Britain. As he secured an agent then the firm reproduced his town's crest in the form of transfers on sheets of paper. After firing the transfer onto the glazed pot, a paintress would hand-paint the crest. Adolphus was away for weeks on end,

The inside of one of the bottle ovens.

Ashfield Lodge, formerly the home of W.H. Goss, which stands next to the main factory building.

travelling by rail, steamer, carriage and boat, whichever was the quickest route, to all parts of Britain. Eventually he even went abroad. He wrote nearly every day to his wife Nelly, and told her where to send her next letter to him in each epistle. On his journeys he sketched and took photographs and from these evolved the factory's porcelain historic named models and transfers of scenes. Some of his letters still exist and from these we have been able to trace his routes and his methods of obtaining agents and coats-of-arms. He had a good sense of humour like his father, and his letters contain some amusing sketches of scenes and incidents which took his fancy.

In 1893 the production of Goss cottages began, fully coloured and faithfully reproduced from the original buildings, down to the last timber and ivy branch. These were popular then, and are very much sought after today by the current generation of crestologists, the name now used to describe Goss and crested china collectors.

By 1900 William had left the running of the firm to his sons Adolphus (who called himself 'Goss Boss' much to the annoyance of his father), Victor and Huntley.

What happened to son Godfrey and why he was given a one-way ticket to America by his father will be told in our forthcoming book. His daughters Georgiana, Adeline, Edith and Florence were 'ladies' and did not, of course, work, although it was reckoned that if Adeline could have run the firm she would have saved it.

Between 1880 and 1900 the firm could not produce enough china to meet demand from the evergrowing number of agencies, which eventually exceeded one thousand, and so to help meet the fantastic demand, the sons decided to enlarge the floor space and take on new staff. Although William did not agree with this, he had retired to his home and lived like a recluse. He concentrated upon the writing of his books, and did not stand in the way of progress. The improvements were carried out between 1902 and 1905. A new 3 storey warehouse was completed by 1904, being linked to the original warehouse which had a stone Gosshawk high up in the wall, by a bridge. Also that year three biscuit ovens were completed and in the following year extra enamelling kilns, two large glost ovens for glazing and another two-storey building with a basement. William never set foot in any of these new buildings, simply because he did not approve of any form of mass production. He also did not care for such ungentlemanly things as advertising, or printed matter such as *The Goss Records*, which J.J. Jarvis worked hard at getting William's permission to publish. There is no doubt that he was much too conservative ever to be in 'big business', and it was not surprising that so many other firms competed with him – he left the field so wide open!

William died in 1906, leaving Adolphus money in his will instead of a share in the firm. We now know the reason for his fall from grace in his father's eyes and, once again, will tell all in our forthcoming book about W.H. Goss, his

The Goss Agency at Mundesley, Norfolk, photographed around 1915. Note the cabinet display of Goss China and agent's sign on the extreme left.

Virtually every town in the land sported a Goss Agency. Some, like this one at St. Leonards-on-Sea, were still advertising enthusiastically as late as 1929.

family and his work. Victor and Huntley were now in charge of the manufacturing and carried on as their father would have wished, with the exception of their commencing advertising one month after his death! Captain Victor Goss, who had been his father's favourite, unfortunately died in a riding accident in 1913 and left Huntley to manage the works alone. Victor's loss was a great one to the factory. As well as a good businessman he was a well respected, likeable gentleman, and was responsible for most of the new models introduced between 1906 and 1913, all of them in good taste. He had served in the Boer War in 1901–2 and was famous locally for his horsemanship and his fashionable taste in clothes and cars.

(William) Huntley, who bore his father's initials but did not inherit his business acumen, had to suffer the First World War in sole charge of the works, with many of his staff and customers on war service and many of the foreign agencies now beyond reach. Then came the depression of the Thirties, and his inability to move with the times led to the firm's downfall. He would not, for instance, have a telephone installed. His heraldic ware remained as perfect as his father would have wished right up until the end, with no short cuts or loss of quality. It must be stressed that the Goss firm did not go into liquidation. Huntley ensured that every bill and every wage was paid before he sold out to Cauldon Potteries in 1929. After this date wares were mainly marked 'W.H. Goss England'. These included brightly coloured figurines in the Doulton style called 'Flower Girls' and pottery. Some of the last products were manufactured to commemorate the 1938 Scottish Empire Exhibition in Glasgow. George Jones owned Cauldon, and the works traded under such names as 'W.H. Goss Ltd', and 'The Goss China Co. Ltd'.

In 1930 the firm went into liquidation because the then owner, Harold Taylor Robinson, had overstretched himself in his efforts to control as many potteries as he could purchase.

The firm was eventually sold to The Coalport China Co. in 1945. Ridgeway and Adderley took them over in 1954, and they were eventually taken over by Royal Doulton.

Marks on W.H. Goss China

MARKS ON W.H. GOSS CHINA

In general, there are two basic types of mark, the W.H. Goss impressed mark, with or sans serif, and the Gosshawk. These appear on some 90% of pieces found and this makes Goss collecting relatively easy. Some items bear only an impressed mark, some only the Gosshawk and some both. None of these variations have any bearing on price any more than does the age of a piece, in spite of what you might be told by some dealers anxious to sell their wares any way they can!

Over the years, various markings have been used by the factory, by far the commonest being the Gosshawk with the name W.H. GOSS below it. Goss himself alleged that this mark was in use continuously from 1862, but some doubt exists as many items, both glazed and unglazed, made after this date were not so marked.

To take the subject chronologically, from 1858 until the introduction of the Gosshawk mark, an impressed W.H. GOSS should appear somewhere on the item. This impressed mark continues to be used haphazardly right up to at least 1916 on some items which also bore the Gosshawk mark. Certain early items have been found with merely an impressed W.H.G., a variation.

The impressed W.H. GOSS can also be found in a type-face with serifs – viz: **W.H. GOSS** – on earlier pieces, and in sans-serif type – viz: **W.H. GOSS** – on later ones. Both types of marking were used in 1887, and so, unless both dies were used concurrently, which is quite possible, this may be considered a further way of dating items.

An alternative identification in the earlier days was the incision, in longhand, of certain details, an example of which reads:

Published as the Act directs (See 54.Geo.III.C 56.)

W. H. Goss.

Stoke-on-Trent.

1 Dec 1873.

Copyright

Minor variations in this wording occur.

This identification became standard when used on the majority of the Parian busts, figures and groups produced during the middle 1870's through to 1911. It was either stamped into the still-wet porcelain or transfer-printed onto the finished piece in black, and reads:

Copyright as Act directs
W. H. GOSS.
Stoke-on-Trent.
1 November 1881.

or, more fully:

Copyright
Pub. as Act Directs
(See 54. Geo III. C 56)
W. H. GOSS.
Stoke-on-Trent.
22 Jany 1893.

The above markings are particularly interesting as they incorporate the publication date, which is not necessarily, of course, the date of manufacture of that particular piece.

It is difficult, owing to its scarcity, to be definite about terracotta ware, but items are known either with the "Copyright as The Act directs . . ." impressed marking, and also with a plain black W H GOSS. Items marked, incised or impressed GOSS & PEAKE are rare, and relate to the short-lived partnership with Mr. Peake.

From around 1862 until about 1930, the Gosshawk and W. H. GOSS marking, sometimes accompanied by an impressed W.H. GOSS was used.

From about 1930 until about 1939, the Gosshawk and W. H. GOSS appears, usually with the word ENGLAND added beneath it. The previous marking continued in use occasionally on some of these later items at least until the time of the Empire Exhibition held in Scotland in 1938.

Pieces bearing the added titles *Cottage Pottery*, *Royal Buff* and *Hand-Painted* must be considered to have originated between about 1925 and 1939, and the addition of the word ENGLAND indicates their being made after about 1930.

During these later years, a rubber stamp was also used for identification. Somewhat larger than, but similar to, the normal marking, being some 17mm wide and 16mm high, it appears mainly on lustre items. It dates from 1925 and continued in use until the demise of the works in the early 30's.

In addition to identification markings, a number of models carry Registration numbers. Registration of models or designs commenced in 1884, and continued until the outbreak of war in 1914. Models bearing the transfer-printed word 'Copyright' may be safely assumed to have been introduced during or after the First World War.

Perhaps this is an appropriate place to dispel two popular misconceptions, both of which have appeared in authoritative books on porcelain and antiques.

Firstly, that "The impressed W. H. GOSS was only placed on perfect

Incised inscription on large bust in W.H. Goss' own hand

Black printed mark, 1867

Black detailed printed mark on Figurine, 1867

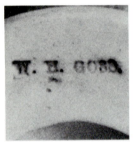

Serif impressed mark 1858–1887 approximately

Serif impressed mark 1858—1887 approximately

Black printed mark on terra-cotta

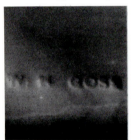

Sans-serif impressed mark 1887—1916 approximately

Serif impressed mark 1887—1918 approximately Stamped mark with registration date

Longhand impressed in W.H. Goss' own hand

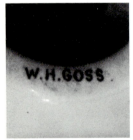

Printed mark on Pepper Pot 1895–1925

The normal Gosshawk 1862–1927

Printed mark on a bust

22

Gosshawk showing
Registration mark

Gosshawk, registration
number and agents name

League model inscription.
Note the artists mark

Goss England mark on a
Flower Girl. Note also the
Artists Mark.

Very late Gosshawk mark.
Probably Post 1930

Post 1930 late mark

Large rubber stamp
Gosshawk 1925 and after

Royal Cauldon mark
over-printed by a Gosshawk.
Post 1925

Impressed mark on a Goss doll
1920–1930 approximately

W.H. Goss England Cottage
Pottery mark

W.H. Goss England Royal
Buff mark

W.H. Goss England hand
painted late mark

products". As this mark would have to be made into the soft clay before even its first firing in the kiln, this is clearly incorrect.

Secondly, that if the word ENGLAND appears beneath the Goshawk and W. H. GOSS mark, then that item was made after 1891, and that consequently items bearing the earlier mark must have been produced before 1891. It was from 1891 that English porcelain manufacturers were supposed to indicate on their wares the country of origin. The truth of the matter, as far as Goss was concerned, is that this instruction was ignored, and it was only export items that were marked MADE IN ENGLAND – or IMPORTE D'ANGLE-TERRE.

As will be noted above, the ENGLAND addition commenced around 1930.

Notes for the Collector

MINOR VARIATIONS IN SIZE

Where the dimensions of items are given, these have been obtained from actual specimens and refer to the height unless otherwise stated. Where an approximate measurement is quoted, no immediate specimen has been to hand, and the best available information source has been used.

Where no dimension is given, it has not proved possible to gain access to information other than to confirm the existence of that model.

With regard to slight fluctuations in size in the same model, it must be borne in mind that variations in the firing temperatures may give rise to these variations, and, in any case, shrinkage in firing can be as high as ten per cent. In early Goss items this figure is said to be higher, and certainly early wares have a tendency to firing-cracks and flaws which the factory seems to have later overcome. So if you have two Rufus Stones that differ by 5mm in height, please do not worry about it!

Examples of items particularly prone to having many minor differences in size are Loving Cups, Wall Pockets and Busts.

Early pieces tend to be heavier and less perfectly rounded than later pieces. Gilding tends to come off at the slightest rub and a heavy mould line is often apparent.

It was not until 1890–1900 that quality was improved by perfecting the moulding technique so ensuring a thinner, more precise model. Gilding was of better quality and it stayed on. Greater colour and precision in the application of coats-of-arms was apparent and after these improvements had been made the pieces were as fine as they would ever be.

CLAY PIPES, TEETH and BUTTONS

A Mr. Angel of Hendon, London, acquired the Goss factory in 1947 and later sold it to Washington Potteries (China Craft) Ltd. in 1951.

Prior to taking possession of his newly acquired premises, Mr. Angel was told they had been used for storage and this would seem to be the case as the building was littered with moulds (all later destroyed) and assorted products in various stages of manufacture. Indeed the new owner remembers seeing large quantities of multi-coloured toby jugs, birds and animals.

A huge unopened post, contained many orders, including a number from the United States and Central Africa.

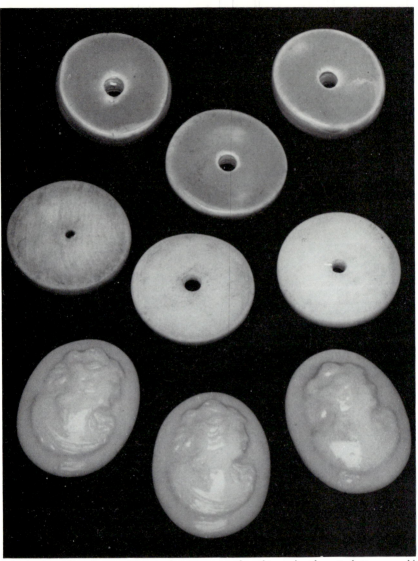

A selection of Goss Buttons. Those in the top row are coloured turquoise, the centre buttons are white glazed and in the bottom row are three imitation cameos in relief.

It appears that the Goss factory had built up a considerable export business in traditional long-stemmed clay pipes so popular with farmers of the Mid-West; in fact, these were a main feature of a Calendar produced by the Goss factory as an advertisement, while the Southern States found the gaudy colours of Goss England ladies, toby jugs and animals to their taste.

The most incredible sales of all however, were the bulk orders of china "teeth" etc. for natives of Africa to make up into necklaces etc., the supplies of the real thing having become almost unobtainable due to the abolition of cannibalism.

A range of buttons was produced, all unmarked, but William Huntley Goss considered them a failure and production was experimental only. This is a pity as the factory produced a cameo button of particularly fine quality.

No price is put on these items and it is not known even if any were marked, but they may be, so always remember to look!

FORGERIES

Very few forgeries of Goss china have appeared. Those that have usually take the form of a forged Gosshawk on a piece that clearly did not originate from the Goss factory. These Gosshawks are either crudely rubber stamped or drawn in Indian Ink. The giveaway must always be the quality of the piece the mark appears on. If it is not the fine perfect parian body that is consistent with Goss then look very closely at the mark. If possible compare a possible forgery with a correct normal mark, compare the quality of the porclain also.

In the end however, recognition of forgeries rests with the experience and the knowledge of the collector and there can be no substitute for handling Goss as often as possible in order to familiarize oneself with the ware.

Occasionally forged cottages appear. All Goss cottages produced are listed in the appropriate chapter in this book. Any other cottage which purports to be Goss is most definitely not so, if it does not feature in the exhaustive list given. Shakespeare's Cottage is a particular exception as so many sizes were produced by both Goss and other crested manufacturers. A forged example has been found of the half-sized, solid base model as well as the 105mm full length size. The latter cottage is well made and is only prevented from being condemned as a true forgery by carrying the inscription 'Reproduction of Model of Shakespeare's House'. It carries the correct registration number and the usual Gosshawk so look for the words 'Reproduction of' in this case.

THE BLACKPOOL COAT OF ARMS

Presumably at the request of the then Blackpool Agent, the Blackpool coat-of-arms was placed on a number of items which would not normally carry a coat-of-arms. Collectors may find it a little distracting to be faced with Blackpool on, for instance, a Manx Cottage, a Lincoln Imp, a St. Columb

Major Cross, a Lucerne Lion, a Goss Oven, or even a Cornish Stile, and these are only a few of the examples that may be found.

Another feature of Mr. Naylor, the Blackpool Agent at the time, was the sale of named models from which the descriptive matter had been omitted. This, together with an over-generous use of gilding (e.g. on the ears of the Lincoln Imp) has tended to give some collectors the impression that Blackpool wares are second-rate, and should be generally avoided. Almost all, however, that was sold through the Blackpool Agency, which changed hands at least four times between the years 1901 and 1921, was perfectly normal and correct.

No collection can be considered really complete without an example of these oddities – while the more staunch Blackpudlians may even consider trying to specialize in these wares.

Price-wise, it is felt that items which should not be carrying arms, but are found to have the Blackpool coat-of-arms tends to detract, reducing the value of the item by, say, between one third and two thirds.

However, many items which would otherwise have been factory rejects (by virtue of firing flaws, distortions, etc.,) have been sold through the Blackpool agency and therefore carry the Blackpool arms. Such pieces would be worth around one-third of the normal perfect model and every Blackpool crested item should therefore be closely inspected in order to determine whether or not it was a factory second.

REGISTRATION NUMBERS

No piece of Goss is worth any more or less whether it carries a registration number or not. There is no reason why some pieces carry their number and some not, the production of Goss china was never an exact science and the only reason for putting the registration number on a piece was to prevent other firms from using the design.

Two different things were registered. Firstly, the shape or model and, secondly, the decoration. Some pieces have one number which could refer to either and some carry two numbers indicating that both the model and decoration were designed and registered by the Goss factory. Registration numbers were not used by the factory after July 1914, but it should also be remembered that a number tells us only when the registration took place, not when the piece was made which might well be years afterwards.

Registration numbers were used from 1884 until they were discontinued in 1914. The following tables gives the dates of first registration of numbers between 1 and 630174. It should be noted that the dates given here indicate only the first registration of a design and not the exact year of manufacture.

Rd No   1   registered in Jan. 1884
Rd No 19754   registered in Jan. 1885
Rd No 40480   registered in Jan. 1886

Rd No   64520 registered in Jan. 1887
Rd No   90483 registered in Jan. 1888
Rd No 116648 registered in Jan. 1889
Rd No 141273 registered in Jan. 1890
Rd No 163767 registered in Jan. 1891
Rd No 185713 registered in Jan. 1892
Rd No 205240 registered in Jan. 1893
Rd No 224720 registered in Jan. 1894
Rd No 246975 registered in Jan. 1895
Rd No 268392 registered in Jan. 1896
Rd No 291241 registered in Jan. 1897
Rd No 311658 registered in Jan. 1898
Rd No 331707 registered in Jan. 1899
Rd No 351202 registered in Jan. 1900
Rd No 368154 registered in Jan. 1901

First Registration No. for 1902   385088
First Registration No. for 1903   402913
First Registration No. for 1904   424017
First Registration No. for 1905   447548
First Registration No. for 1906   471486
First Registration No. for 1907   493487
First Registration No. for 1908   518415
First Registration No. for 1909   534963
First Registration No. for 1910   554801
First Registration No. for 1911   575787
First Registration No. for 1912   594182
First Registration No. for 1913   612382
First Registration No. for 1914   603174

Named Models
and Special Shapes

This chapter is probably the most important, as it contains the six hundred or so models which are the most avidly collected products of the Goss factory. Cottages, Fonts, Animals and Crosses are also models, but due to their importance, will be found under their own classifications.

League and International League of Goss Collectors models will be found under this section and it should be noted that with the exception of the Portland Vase, they only appear with either of the two league decorations.

Two prices are given in this chapter, one for pieces with any arms and the second for those with Matching Arms. For example an Abergavenny Jar with Abergavenny arms will be worth more than an example with, say, City of London arms.

No general percentage addition can be added for Matching Arms as particular examples vary so much. It is preferable to have the correct Matching Arms on a model and the following policy has been observed in stating what are considered to be the most appropriate Coats-of-Arms:

(1) If there are Arms of the town or location available, then these would take preference. Where any difficulty arises reference has been made to *The Goss Record* and the correct arms as given have been taken. In cases where there is apparently no correct arms then those of the local agent who was the main agent for that model have been taken. For example, the arms of New Milton, the local agency, are considered correct for the Ashley Rails Urn, but any nearby town would be local.
(2) If a model relates to a specific person, then the Arms of that person (if available) is to be preferred.

In the absence of an 'exact' match, the following would be considered "correct", and 10% to 50% to the basic value should be added.

(1) The Arms of the county in which a town lies, or the town seal or other motif.
(2) The Arms of any Cathedral, School, Hospital, or famous person etc., relating to that town.

Most pieces have arms that attract higher prices than others. For example, *any* Welsh arms on a Welsh model would be worth the matching price in full as these models relate to the principality as a whole and not just to one town. (This only applies to models commencing with the word 'Welsh'.) Similarly, *any* Swiss arms on a Swiss model are considered matching but where a model relates to a particular town, the arms of that town take precedence. Other local places and the relevant county will attract the premium previously stated.

Some pieces are listed with only one price. This is where the item is known only with or without matching arms as the case may be. For example, the Hawkins Henley Scull appears only with the matching arms of Henley-on-Thames and so no price is given for a variety without arms.

Models which do not normally bear any arms at all are priced in the first column. Such pieces are marked with a dagger thus: †

All dimensions refer to the height unless otherwise stated.

Model			With any Arms £ p	With Matching Arms £ p
for ABBOT BEERE'S JACK see Glastonbury (Abbot Beere's) Jack				
for ABBOTS CUP, FOUNTAINS ABBEY see Fountains Abbey, Abbot's Cup				
ABERDEEN BRONZE POT		63mm	4.50	8.25
(Goss Record. 8th Edition. Page 4)		89mm	6.50	12.50
also see Chapter headed 'POSTCARDS'		133mm	24.50	30.00
Matching Arms: ABERDEEN				
ABERGAVENNY ANCIENT JAR		54mm	4.00	8.00
(Goss Record. 8th Edition. Page 29)				
Matching Arms: ABERGAVENNY				
ABINGDON ROMAN VASE		95mm	14.50	22.50
(Goss Record. 8th Edition: Page 16)				
Matching Arms: ABINGDON				
ACANTHUS ROSE BOWL	and wire cage	130mm	65.00	
	without wire cage	130mm	47.00	
(Goss Record. 8th Edition: Page 45) This model was originally sold with a wire cage. *It has no correct arms.*				
ALDERNEY FISH BASKET		40mm		25.00
(Goss Record. 8th Edition. Page 17)		58mm		30.00
Matching Arms: ALDERNEY				
ALDERNEY MILK CAN (and lid)		70mm		26.50
Matching Arms: ALDERNEY		108mm		30.00
This model has a lid without which it is		140mm		32.50
incomplete. Value approximately £7.00				

Aberdeen Bronze Pot

Abergavenny Jar

Abingdon Roman Vase

Acanthus Rose Bowl

Alderney Fish Basket

Alderney Milk Can and Lid

Alnwick Celtic Sepulchral Urn

Amersham Leaden Measure

Ancient Costril

Arundel Roman Ewer

Antwerp Oolen Pot

Appleby Elizabethan Bushel Measure

Model		With any Arms £ p	With Matching Arms £ p
ALNWICK CELTIC SEPULCHRAL URN	68mm	7.00	10.50
(Goss Record. 8th Edition. Page 30) *Matching Arms: ALNWICK*			
AMERSHAM LEADEN MEASURE	48mm	7.50	13.00
(Goss Record. 8th Edition. Page 17) *Matching Arms: AMERSHAM*			

for AMPHORA VASE
see Greek Amphora Vase or Domestic and
ornamental chapter

ANCIENT COSTRIL	56mm(a)		30.00
(Goss Record. 9th Edition. Pages 22, 28, 40 and Plate B)	56mm(b)		35.00

This model was first introduced bearing the League of
Goss Collectors Motif (a) and re-introduced later
bearing the International Legue of Goss Collectors Motif (b).

for ANCIENT STONE VESSEL, DOVER CASTLE
see Dover Mortar

for ANCIENT TYG (One Handle)
see Staffordshire One Handled Tyg

for ANCIENT TYG (Two Handles)
see Staffordshire Two Handled Tyg

for ANGLO-SAXON CINERARY URN
see King's Newton Anglo-Saxon Cinerary Urn

ANTWERP OOLEN POT with 1 coat of arms	70mm	4.50	8.25
with 3 coats of arms	70mm	6.50	11.50
(Goss Record. 8th Edition. Page 42) *Matching Arms: ANTWERPEN*			

APPLEBY ELIZABETHAN BUSHEL MEASURE			
(Goss Record. 8th Edition: Page 36)	Dia. 59mm	11.00	19.50
Matching Arms: APPLEBY			

ARUNDEL ROMAN EWER	55mm	6.00	13.00
	102mm	10.50	16.00
(Goss Record. 8th Edition: Page 34) *Matching Arms: ARUNDEL*			

ASHBOURNE BUSHEL	Dia. 51mm	7.50	16.00
(Goss Record. 8th Edition: Page 18) *Matching Arms: ASHBOURNE*			

Model			With any Arms £ p	With Matching Arms £ p
ASHLEY RAILS ROMAN URN This model is marked "copyright" *Matching Arms: NEW MILTON*		108mm	26.00	35.00
for ASHMOLEAN VASE, GNOSSUS see Gnossus Ashmolean Vase				
for ATWICK VASE see Hornsea Roman Vase				
AVEBURY CELTIC URN (Goss Record. 8th Edition: Page 36) *Matching Arms: CALNE, MARLBOROUGH or DEVIZES*		105mm	11.00	15.25
for AYSGILL URN see Hawes Ancient British Urn				
(CUP OF) BALLAFLETCHER The Llannan Shee (Peaceful Spirit) (Goss Record. 8th Edition: Page 24) *Matching Arms: DOUGLAS, ISLE OF MAN*		95mm	21.75	40.00
for BARGATE, SOUTHAMPTON see Southampton, Bargate				
BARNET STONE (Goss Record. 8th Edition: Page 24)	(a) White † (b) Brown †	172mm 172mm	85.00 125.00	
BARTLOW EWER (Goss Record. 8th Edition: Page 22) *Matching Arms: SAFFRON WALDEN*		104mm	16.50	22.50
BATH ANCIENT ROMAN CUP (Goss Record. 8th Edition: Page 31) *Matching Arms: BATH*		102mm	75.00	110.00
BATH BRONZE ROMAN EWER see also Chapter headed 'Postcards' (Goss Record. 8th Edition: Page 31) *Matching Arms: BATH*		120mm	15.50	22.50
BATH ROMAN EWER (Goss Record. 8th Edition: Page 31) *Matching Arms: BATH*		63mm 130mm	3.50 10.50	7.50 19.50

Ashbourne Bushel

Ashley Rails Roman Urn

Avebury Celtic Urn

(Cup of) Ballafletcher

*Barnet Stone
White and Brown*

Bartlow Ewer

Bath Roman Cup

Bath Bronze Roman Ewer

Bath Roman Ewer

Bath Roman Jug

Bath Roman Urn

Beachy Head Lighthouse

35

Model		With any Arms £ p	With Matching Arms £ p
BATH ROMAN JUG	150mm	19.50	28.50
(Goss Record. 8th Edition: Page 31)			
Matching Arms: BATH			
for **BATTLE OF LARGS MEMORIAL TOWER**			
see Largs Memorial Tower			
BEACHY HEAD LIGHTHOUSE (a) Brown band	125mm	30.00	40.00
(Goss Record. 8th Edition: Page 34) (b) Black band	125mm	30.00	40.00
Matching Arms: EASTBOURNE			
It is interesting to note that this exact model also			
appears as the extremely rare DUNGENESS			
LIGHTHOUSE			
BECCLES RINGER'S JUG	87mm		275.00
Very rare, has only been seen bearing matching arms.			
Matching Arms: ANCIENT SEAL OF BECCLES			
BETTWS-Y-COED ANCIENT BRONZE KETTLE	73mm	8.75	14.50
(Goss Record. 8th Edition: Page 38)	114mm	16.00	21.50
Matching Arms: BETTWS-Y-COED			
BIDEFORD ANCIENT MORTAR	42mm	8.00	12.50
(Goss Record. 8th Edition: Page 20)			
Matching Arms: BIDEFORD			
for **BLACK AND BROWN CUP**			
see Newcastle (Staffordshire) Cup			
BLACKGANG CANNON	Length	6.50	12.50
(Goss Record. 8th Edition: Page 26)	95mm		
Matching Arms: BLACKGANG			
BLACKGANG TOWER, ST. CATHERINE'S HILL	112mm	21.75	30.00
(Goss Record. 8th Edition: Page 26)			
Matching Arms: BLACKGANG			
BLACKPOOL TOWER	118mm	28.50	35.00
(Goss Record. 9th Edition: Page 21 & Platge J)			
Matching Arms: BLACKPOOL			
BOGNOR LOBSTER TRAP (identical to	51mm		52.50
Lobster Trap but specifically named)			
Matching Arms: BOGNOR			

Beccles Ringers Jug

Bettys-y-Coed kettle

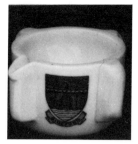
Bideford Mortar

Blackgang Cannon

Blackgang Tower

Blackpool Tower

Bognor Regis Lobster Trap

Bolton Abbey Wine Cooler

Boston Ancient Ewer

Boulogne Milk Can & Lid

Boulogne Sedan Chair

Boulogne Wooden Shoe

*Bournemouth Bronze
Mace Head*

*Bournemouth Ancient
Egyptian Lamp*

*Bournemouth Pilgrim
Bottle*

Bournemouth Pine Cone

*Bournemouth Bronze
Urn*

Brading Stocks

Brading Roman Ewer

Braunton Lighthouse

(The nose of) Brazenose

*Bridlington Quart
Measure*

Bristol Puzzle Cider Cup

British 6" Incendiary Shell

Model		With any Arms £ p	With Matching Arms £ p
BOLTON ABBEY WINE COOLER (Goss Record. 8th Edition: Page 38) *Matching Arms: BOLTON ABBEY*	Dia. 68mm	14.50	24.50
BOSTON ANCIENT EWER (Goss Record. 8th Edition: Page 28) *Matching Arms: BOSTON*	70mm	5.50	11.50
BOULOGNE MILK CAN (and lid) (Goss Record. 8th Edition: Page 42) *Matching Arms: BOULOGNE-SUR-MER* The model is incomplete without its lid, value £8.00	74mm	10.50	25.75
BOULOGNE SEDAN CHAIR (Goss Record. 8th Edition: Page 42) In the 8th Edition of the Goss Record (Page 1) a version 'specially' decorated in Turquoise Blue is advertised (b). This model has very fragile handles, even with one of these broken it would be almost worthless. *Matching Arms: BOULOGNE-SUR-MER*	(a) 69mm (b) 69mm	34.50 200.00	65.00
BOULOGNE WOODEN SHOE (Goss Record. 8th Edition: Page 42) *Matching Arms: BOULOGNE-SUR-MER*	Length 118mm	16.50	40.00
BOURNEMOUTH ANCIENT BRONZE MACE HEAD (Goss Record. 8th Edition: Page 22) *Matching Arms: BOURNEMOUTH*	80mm	11.50	17.50
BOURNEMOUTH ANCIENT EGYPTIAN LAMP (Goss Record. 8th Edition: Page 23) *Matching Arms: BOURNEMOUTH*	Length 105mm	13.00	19.50
BOURNEMOUTH PILGRIM BOTTLE (Goss Record. 8th Edition: Page 23) *Matching Arms: BOURNEMOUTH*	90mm	8.75	11.00
BOURNEMOUTH PINE CONE (Goss Record. 8th Edition: Page 23) *Matching Arms: BOURNEMOUTH*	90mm	8.00	10.50
BOURNEMOUTH BRONZE URN (Goss Record. 8th Edition: Page 23) *Matching Arms: BOURNEMOUTH*	52mm	6.50	9.00

Model		With any Arms £ p	With Matching Arms £ p
BRADING STOCKS This model is marked 'copyright' *Matching Arms: ARMS or SEAL OF BRADING*	Length 87mm	200.00	280.00
BRADING ROMAN EWER (Goss Record. 8th Edition: Page 26) Also known as the Isle of Wight Roman Ewer by J.J. Jarvis in the Goss Record. As it is not so named on the piece itself we prefer to call it the Brading Ewer. *Either BRADING or ISLE OF WIGHT may be considered as Matching Arms.*	(a) 70mm (b)125mm	5.50 8.75	11.00 14.50
for 'BRAMPTON WARE' MUG see Chesterfield 'Brampton Ware' Mug			
BRAUNTON LIGHTHOUSE The second rarest lighthouse, it has a grey roof. *Matching Arms: WESTWARD HO*	133mm	380.00	450.00
(THE NOSE OF) BRASENOSE (Goss Record. 8th Edition: Page 31) Brasenose is frequently spelt Brazenose but for the purpose of this publication the example of the Goss Record is faithfully followed. *The Matching Arms are BRAZENOSE or THE CITY OF OXFORD*	104mm	14.00	22.50
for (OLD) BRAZIER AT TRESCO see Tresco Old Brazier			
BRIDLINGTON ELIZABETHAN QUART **MEASURE** (Goss Record. 8th Edition: Page 38) *Matching Arms: BRIDLINGTON*	50mm	6.50	12.50
BRISTOL PUZZLE CIDER CUP (Goss Record. 8th Edition: Page 22) *Matching Arms: BRISTOL*	51mm	12.50	21.50
for BRITISH CONTACT MINE or BRITISH SEA MINE see Contact Mine			
BRITISH (SIX INCH) SHELL (Goss Record. World War Edition. Pages 5 [illus- trated] and 7). This model is marked 'copyright'. The value of any military crest is to be added to the price, say £10 – £45 depending upon rarity and suitability. *Correct Arms: Any Artillery Regiment*	110mm	14.50	

British Tank

Brixworth Ancient Cup

Broadway Tower

Burton Beer Barrel

Bury St. Edmunds Bomb

*Bury St. Edmunds Libation
Vessel and Lid*

Caerhun Urn

*Caerleon Lachrymatory or
Tear Bottle*

Caerleon Lamp

Cambridge Pitcher

Cambridge Roman Jug

Canary Porron

41

Model			With any Arms £ p	With Matching Arms £ p
BRITISH TANK		Length	30.00	
(Goss Record. 9th Edition: Plate L)		110mm		
This model is marked 'copyright'.				
Matching Arms: (a) LINCOLN				47.50
(b) ROYAL TANK CORPS				65.00
BRIXWORTH ANCIENT CUP		55mm	4.50	8.00
(Goss Record. 8th Edition: Page 30)				
Matching Arms: NORTHAMPTON (SHIRE)				
BROADWAY TOWER	(a) White	75mm	110.00	175.00
(Goss Record. 8th Edition: Page 36)	(b) Grey †	75mm	190.00	
	(c) Brown †	75mm	250.00	
Matching Arms: BROADWAY				
BURTON BEER BARREL		60mm	6.00	11.50
(Goss Record. 8th Edition: Page 32)		73mm	7.50	12.00
Matching Arms: BURTON-ON-TRENT				
BURY ST. EDMUNDS GERMAN BOMB		75mm	17.50	24.50
(Goss Record. 9th Edition: Page 28)				
This model is marked 'copyright' and has an extremely delicate handle, without which it is of little value.				
Matching Arms: BURY ST. EDMUNDS				
BURY ST. EDMUNDS KETTLE (and lid)		76mm	10.50	16.00
(Goss Record. 8th Edition: Page 34)		121mm	17.50	24.50
This model is not complete without its lid.				
Matching Arms: BURY ST. EDMUNDS				

for BURY ST. EDMUNDS LIBATION VESSEL
see Bury St. Edmunds Kettle

for CAERHUN BRONZE CROCHON
see Welsh Crochon

CAERHUN URN	54mm	15.00	26.00

This model is marked 'copyright'.
Probably the rarest of the smaller urns.
Matching Arms: CONWAY

Model		With any Arms £ p	With Matching Arms £ p

CAERLEON GLASS LACHRYMATORY
  (or tear bottle) — 86mm — 5.50
(Goss Record. 8th Edition: Page 29)
Matching Arms: (a) CAERLEON — 15.25
            (b) NEWPORT — 13.00

CAERLEON LAMP — Length
(Goss Record. 8th Edition: Page 29) — 88mm — 5.50
Matching Arms: (a) CAERLEON — 12.00
            (b) NEWPORT — 7.50

for CAERLEON TEAR BOTTLE
see Caerleon Glass Lachrymatory

CAMBRIDGE PITCHER — 63mm — 3.50 — 6.50
(Goss Record. 8th Edition: Page 17) — 108mm — 7.00 — 11.00
Matching Arms: CAMBRIDGE

CAMBRIDGE ROMAN JUG — 76mm — 7.50 — 11.00
This model is not to be found named in the usual way. — 88mm — 9.50 — 12.00
However, the illustration of the model on a Trent — 94mm — 11.00 — 16.00
Postcard is ample evidence of its status. (See also — 120mm — 28.00 — 32.50
TERRA COTTA) — 145mm — 30.00 — 40.00
Matching Arms: CAMBRIDGE

for CANARY ANCIENT COVERED JARRA
see Las Palmas Ancient Covered Jarra

for CANARY ANCIENT EARTHEN JAR
see Las Palmas Ancient Earthen Jar

for CANARY ANCIENT JARRA
see Las Palmas Ancient Jarra

CANARY PORRON — 68mm — 21.00 — 32.50
(Goss Record. 8th Edition: Page 42)
This model is identical to the Gibraltar Alcaraza – pick
them all up and check the wording, you may be lucky.
Matching Arms: LAS PALMAS, GRAND CANARY

for CANNON BALL
see Rye Cannon Ball

Canterbury Jug

Canterbury Leather Bottle

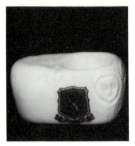

Capel Madoc Stoup

Cardinal Beaufort's Candlestick

Cardinal Beaufort's Salt Cellar

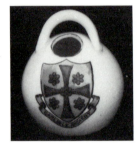

Carlisle Salt Pot

Carmarthen Coracle

Carnarvon Ewer

Castletown Cinerary Urn

The Cenotaph, Whitehall

Cheddar Cheese

Cherbourg Milk Can and Lid

Model		With any Arms £ p	With Matching Arms £ p
CANTERBURY JUG (Goss Record. 8th Edition: Page 26) Early models merely state: 'The Canterbury Jug' *Matching Arms: CANTERBURY*	113mm	8.00	11.00
CANTERBURY LEATHER BOTTLE (Goss Record. 8th Edition: Page 26) *Matching Arms: CANTERBURY*	46mm	3.25	6.50
CAPEL MADOC STOUP (Goss Record. 9th Edition: Page 34) *Matching Arms: RHAYADER*	Length 80mm	16.00	26.00
CARDINAL BEAUFORT'S CANDLESTICK (Goss Record. 8th Edition: Page 23) *Matching Arms: CARDINAL BEAUFORT or WINCHESTER*	152mm	95.00	175.00
CARDINAL BEAUFORT'S SALT CELLAR (Goss Record. 8th Edition: Page 23) *Matching Arms: CARDINAL BEAUFORT or WINCHESTER*	70mm	56.50	87.50
CARLISLE OLD SALT POT (Goss Record. 8th Edition: Page 18) *Matching Arms: CARLISLE*	46mm	3.50	6.50
CARMARTHEN CORACLE (Goss Record. 8th Edition: Page 38) *Matching Arms: CARMARTHEN*	Length 133mm	21.75	30.00
CARNARVON EWER (Goss Record. 8th Edition: Page 39) *Matching Arms: CARNARVON*	63mm 89mm	5.25 7.50	8.00 13.00
CASTLETOWN CINERARY URN (Goss Record. 8th Edition: Page 24) *Matching Arms: CASTLETOWN, ISLE OF MAN*	40mm	5.00	8.25
CENOTAPH, WHITEHALL (a) White glazed (b) White unglazed† This model can be found either glazed or unglazed and in various sizes. (See also GOSS ENGLAND) *Matching Arms: CITY OF LONDON*	145mm 145mm	26.00 47.50	30.00

for CHARLOTTE'S (QUEEN) FAVOURITE WINDSOR KETTLE
see Windsor Kettle

Model			With any Arms £ p	With Matching Arms £ p
CHEDDAR CHEESE	(a) Yellow	62mm	21.75†	21.75
(Goss Record. 8th Edition: Page 31)	(b) White glazed	62mm	17.50	21.75
Matching Arms: CHEDDAR				
CHERBOURG MILK CAN (and lid)		65mm	14.50	24.50
(Goss Record. 8th Edition: Page 42)				
This model is not complete without its lid which is worth about £10.00 of the price shown.				
Matching Arms: CHERBOURG				
CHESHIRE ROMAN URN		90mm		280.00
International League Model for 1932.				
Correct Arms: INTERNATIONAL LEAGUE OF GOSS COLLECTORS				
CHESHIRE SALT BLOCK		80mm	17.50	24.50
(Goss Record. 9th Edition: Page 11 and Plate K)				
Matching Arms: CHESHIRE				
CHESTER ROMAN ALTAR		117mm		300.00
International League Model for 1931				
Correct Arms: INTERNATIONAL LEAGUE OF GOSS COLLECTORS				
CHESTER ROMAN VASE		59mm	3.25	6.50
(Goss Record. 8th Edition: Page 17)		89mm	8.75	12.50
see also chapter headed POSTCARDS				
Matching Arms: CHESTER				
CHESTERFIELD 'BRAMPTON WARE' MUG		93mm	35.00	56.50
(Goss Record. 9th Edition Page 13)				
This model is marked 'copyright'				
Matching Arms: CHESTERFIELD				
for CHESTERFIELD MUG				
see Chesterfield 'Brampton Ware' Mug				
CHICHESTER EWER		63mm	3.50	7.00
(Goss Record. 8th Edition: Page 34)				
Matching Arms: CHICHESTER				
CHICHESTER ROMAN URN		81mm	7.50	11.00
(Goss Record. 8th Edition: Page 34)				
Matching Arms: CHICHESTER				

Cheshire Roman Urn

Cheshire Salt Block

Channel Islands Fish Basket

Chester Roman Altar

Chester Roman Vase

Chesterfield 'Brampton Ware' Mug

Chichester Roman Ewer

Chichester Roman Urn

Chile Stirrup

Chile Hat

Chile Mate Cup

Chile Spur

47

Model			With any Arms £ p	With Matching Arms £ p
CHICKEN ROCK LIGHTHOUSE (Goss Record. 8th Edition: Page 26) *Matching Arms: ISLE OF MAN*		127mm	19.50	23.00
CHILE HAT (Goss Record. 9th Edition: Page 37 and Plate 0) *Matching Arms: CHILE*	Dia.	86mm	215.00	350.00
CHILE MATE CUP (Goss Record. 9th Edition: Page 37 and Plate 0) *Matching Arms: CHILE*		60mm	100.00	200.00
CHILE SPUR (Goss Record. 9th Edition: Page 37 and Plate N) *Matching Arms: CHILE*		Length 114mm	200.00	300.00
CHILE STIRRUP (Goss Record. 9th Edition: Page 37 and Plate N) *Matching Arms: CHILE*		50mm	80.00	170.00

for CHIPPING NORTON FOUR SHIRE STONE
see Four Shire Stone

| **CHRISTCHURCH ANCIENT BOWL** (Goss Record. 8th Edition: Page 23 and also see the advertisement for the Christchurch items on page 64) *Matching Arms: CHRISTCHURCH* | Dia. | 60mm | 4.50 | 7.50 |

CHRISTCHURCH PRIORY CHURCH NORMAN TOWER

(Goss Record. 8th Edition: Page 23)	(a) White glazed†	123mm	43.50
	(b) White unglazed†	123mm	43.50
	(c) Grey†	123mm	75.00
	(d) Brown†	123mm	130.00

| **CHRISTCHURCH ROMANO-BRITISH URN** (Goss Record. 8th Edition: Page 23) *Matching Arms: CHRISTCHURCH* | 52mm | 4.00 | 7.50 |

for CHRIST'S HOSPITAL WINE FLAGON
see London Christ's Hospital English Wine Flagon

| **CIRENCESTER ROMAN EWER** (Goss Record. 9th Edition: Pages 22, 41 and Plate c) This model was first introduced bearing the League of Goss Collectors Motif (a) and re-introduced later bearing the International League of Goss Collectors Motif (b). | (a) 78mm (b) 78mm | | 26.00 56.50 |

Model		With any Arms £ p	With Matching Arms £ p
CIRENCESTER ROMAN EWER (a) 2 Crests	115mm	12.50	24.50
(Goss Record. 8th Edition: Page 22) (b) 3 Crests	115mm	14.00	30.00
Matching Arms: CIRENCESTER			
CIRENCESTER ROMAN URN	165mm	87.00	130.00
This model is marked 'copyright' and numbered 784			
(see Roman Vase 783 for comparison)			
Matching Arms: CIRENCESTER			
CIRENCESTER ROMAN VASE	80mm	4.00	7.50
(Goss Record. 8th Edition: Page 22 and	124mm	8.75	10.50
advertisement page 66)			
Matching Arms: CIRENCESTER			
CLIFTONVILLE ROMAN JUG	180mm	175.00	215.00
Matching Arms: MARGATE			
CLIFTONVILLE ROMAN VASE	70mm	150.00	200.00
	107mm	150.00	150.00

Colchester enthusiasts should refer to the Goss Record, 8th Edition: Page 63 for a full page advertisement.

Model		With any Arms £ p	With Matching Arms £ p
COLCHESTER GIGANTIC ROMAN WINE VASE	157mm	24.50	40.00
(Goss Record. 8th Edition: Page 21)			
Matching Arms: COLCHESTER			
COLCHESTER NATIVE OYSTER SHELL	Width	5.50	11.00
(Goss Record. 8th Edition: Page 22)	68mm		
Always appears un-named.			
Matching Arms: COLCHESTER			
COLCHESTER ROMAN LAMP	Length		150.00
International League Model for 1927	100mm		
Matching Arms: INTERNATIONAL LEAGUE OF GOSS			
COLLECTORS			
COLCHESTER VASE (Cloaca) Dia.	65mm	4.00	8.25
(Goss Record. 8th Edition: Page 22)			
Cloaca refers to the place where the original vase			
was found. It is included with the model's name to			
clearly distinguish the piece from the Colchester Vase			
(Famous).			
Matching Arms: COLCHESTER			

Chicken Rock Lighthouse

Christchurch Ancient Bowl

Christchurch Norman Tower

*Christchurch
Romano-British Urn*

*Cirencester Roman Ewer
League Model*

Cirencester Roman Ewer

Cirencester Roman Vase

Cirencester Roman Urn

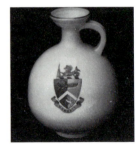
Cliftonville Roman Jug

Cliftonville Roman Vase

*Colchester Gigantic Roman
Wine Vase*

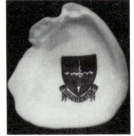
Colchester Oyster Shell

50

Model				With any Arms £ p	With Matching Arms £ p
COLCHESTER ROMAN VASE (Famous)			44mm	3.50	6.50
(Goss Record. 8th Edition: Page 22)			90mm	7.50	11.50
Famous refers to that part of the full name listed in			127mm	9.00	14.50

the Goss Record viz. Famous Roman Colchester Vase. . .
etc. and is quoted to clearly distinguish this model
from the other Colchester Vases.
Matching Arms: COLCHESTER

Model				With any Arms £ p	With Matching Arms £ p
CONTACT MINE			Length		95.00
(Goss Record. 9th Edition: Pages 22, 41 and Plate C)			73mm		

International League Model for 1919.
Correct Arms: INTERNATIONAL LEAGUE OF GOSS
COLLECTORS

Model				With any Arms £ p	With Matching Arms £ p
CORFE CASTLE CUP			62mm	7.00	12.50

(Goss Record. 8th Edition: Page 20)
Matching Arms: CORFE CASTLE

Model				With any Arms £ p	With Matching Arms £ p
CORNISH BUSSA			55mm	4.00	5.50

(Goss Record. 8th Edition: Page 18)
Matching Arms: CORNWALL

CORNISH PASTY

Matching Arms: CORNWALL			With any Arms £ p	With Matching Arms £ p
	(a) White glazed	82mm	43.50	65.00
	(b) Yellow	82mm	65.00	87.50
	(c) White glazed	110mm	43.50	65.00
	(d) Yellow	110mm	65.00	87.50

CORNISH STILE			With any Arms £ p	With Matching Arms £ p
	(a) White unglazed†	Length	40.00	
	(b) White glazed†	72mm	40.00	
	(c) Brown†		65.00	

Variety (b) can be found with the Blackpool arms, which could reduce its value by half.

for CORONATION CHAIR IN WESTMINSTER ABBEY
see Westminster Abbey Coronation Chair

CORONATION CHAIR, PERTH			With any Arms £ p	With Matching Arms £ p
	(a) White glazed	87mm	65.00	87.50
(Goss Record. 9th Edition: Page 36)	(b) Stone in brown	87mm	110.00	130.00
This model is the same as the	(c) Brown†	87mm	240.00	

Westminster Abbey Coronation Chair
except that it carries the following
inscription:
'The chair contains the ancient stone
on which the Kings and Queens of
Scotland were formerly crowned at
Scone, Perthshire.'
Matching Arms: PERTH

Colchester Roman Lamp

Colchester Vase (Cloaca)

Colchester Vase (Famous)

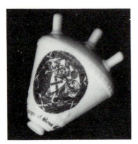
Contact Mine

Corfe Castle Cup

Cornish Bussa

Cornish Pasty

Cornish Stile

*Cuckfield Ancient
Bellarmine*

Cumbrae Monument

Cyprus Myceanaean Vase

Dartmouth Sack Bottle

Model			With any Arms £ p	With Matching Arms £ p

for COSTREL
see Luton Bottle

for CRICKET STONE, HAMBLEDON
see Hambledon Cricket Stone

for CRONK AUST CINERARY URN
see Ramsey Cronk Aust Cinerary Urn

CUCKFIELD ANCIENT BELLARMINE		75mm	7.00	15.25

(Goss Record. 9th Edition: Page 29)
Matching Arms: CUCKFIELD

CUMBRAE MONUMENT, TOWNONTEND				

(Goss Record. 8th Edition: Page 40)   Brown† 175mm   260.00

CYPRUS MYCENAEAN VASE	Dia.	90mm		82.50

International League Model for 1925
*Correct Arms: INTERNATIONAL LEAGUE OF GOSS
    COLLECTORS*

for DART SACK BOTTLE
see Dartmouth Sack Bottle

DARTMOUTH SACK BOTTLE	63mm	4.50	6.50
	82mm	7.50	10.50

(Goss Record. 8th Edition: Page 20)
Matching Arms: DARTMOUTH

DENBIGH BRICK	(a) White glazed	82mm	56.50	87.50
(Goss Record. 8th Edition: Page 39)	(b) White unglazed†	82mm	87.50	
Matching Arms: DENBIGH	(c) Brown or red†	82mm	175.00	

DEVIZES CELTIC DRINKING CUP	63mm	4.50	8.25
	82mm	8.25	10.50

(Goss Record. 8th Edition: Page 36)
Matching Arms: DEVIZES

DEVON CIDER BARREL	60mm	8.75	12.50

This model is marked 'copyright'. It is identical to
the small version of the Burton Beer Barrel but much
rarer. No barrel should be left unturned in future!
Matching Arms: DEVON

Denbigh Brick   *Devizes Celtic Drinking Cup*   *Devon Cider Barrel*

Devon Cooking Pot   *Devon Oak Pitcher*   *Dinant Wooden Shoe*

Doncaster Ewer   *Doncaster Urn*   *Doncaster Vase*

Dorchester Jug   *Dorchester Roman Cup*   *Dorothy Vernon's Porridge Pot*

54

Model		With any Arms £ p	With Matching Arms £ p
DEVON COOKING POT	46mm	8.75	12.50

This model is marked 'copyright'. It is identical to
the Manx Peel Pot but much scarcer . . . be sure to look
at every apparent Peel Pot more closely.
Matching Arms: DEVON

NOTE: These two models are only found with
arms of places in Devonshire. The only truly
correct arms are those of Devon itself.

DEVON PITCHER	59mm	3.25	5.50
(Goss Record. 8th Edition: Page 20)	114mm	12.50	14.50

Matching Arms: DEVON

DINANT WOODEN SHOE	Length	14.50	40.00
(Goss Record. 8th Edition: Page 42)	74mm		

Matching Arms: DINANT

DONCASTER EWER	67mm	9.50	16.00

This model is marked 'copyright'
Matching Arms: DONCASTER

DONCASTER URN	39mm	6.00	11.00

This model is marked 'copyright'
Matching Arms: DONCASTER

DONCASTER VASE	78mm	8.00	13.00

This model is marked 'copyright'
Matching Arms: DONCASTER

DORCHESTER JUG	50mm	3.50	6.50

(Goss Record. 8th Edition: Page 20 and also see full
page advertisement on page 60)
Matching Arms: DORCHESTER

DORCHESTER ROMAN CUP	51mm	3.50	6.50
(Goss Record. 8th Edition: Page 21)	82mm	8.75	12.50

Matching Arms: DORCHESTER

DOROTHY VERNON'S PORRIDGE POT	72mm	7.50	14.50

(Goss Record. 8th Edition: Page 18)
Matching Arms: DOROTHY VERNON

Model		With any Arms £ p	With Matching Arms £ p
DOVER MORTAR (or Stone Vessel)	51mm	4.50	7.50

(Goss Record. 8th Edition: Page 26)
This model is marked on the base 'Ancient Stone
Vessel found at Dover Castle' but it is listed as 'Dover
Mortar' in the 8th Edition (page 26) and 9th Edition
(page 20) of the Goss Record.
Matching Arms: DOVER

DUNGENESS LIGHTHOUSE	125mm		175.00

This model is actually the Beachy Head Lighthouse
re-titled, presumably for the local agent.
The arms on the only example seen have been those of
THE LORDS OF THE LEVEL OF ROMNEY MARSH,
so these may well be considered to be matching.

DURHAM SANCTUARY KNOCKER
(Goss Record. 8th Edition: Page 21)

(a) Flower holder, white	Height 149mm	32.50†	
(b) Flower holder, brown	Height 149mm	37.50†	
(c) Night light	83mm	89.50	110.00
(d) Mug or cup	52mm	35.00	50.00
(e) Mug or cup	80mm	47.00	60.00
(f) Mug or cup	118mm	75.00	87.50

A descriptive leaflet can also be found with the above
items and is worth £10.00
Matching Arms: DURHAM (CATHEDRAL)
An illustration of (c) will be
found on page 160

DUTCH SABOT	Length	12.50	32.50
(Goss Record. 8th Edition: Page 42)	82mm		

Matching Arms: HOLLAND

DUTCH MILK CAN			
(identical to Boulogne Milk Can)	74mm	52.50	70.00

Matching Arms: HOLLAND

EDDYSTONE LIGHTHOUSE	125mm	16.00	21.50

Matching Arms: PLYMOUTH or STONEHOUSE

for EDDYSTONE SPANISH JUG
see Plymouth Jug

for EDINBURGH CASTLE, MONS MEG
see Mons Meg, Edinburgh Castle

Model	With any Arms £ p	With Matching Arms £ p

THE EGYPTIAN MODELS

In order that the Egyptian models may be satisfactorily covered they have been listed in their chronological order of manufacture. According to the 8th Edition of the Goss Record (page 42) models of the Egyptian Water Jar (and the Great Pyramid) were in the course of preparation at the time of going to press (1913). By the time the 9th Edition was published these two models had been on sale for some time (page 37) and ten other models of ancient shapes were listed as being "in preparation".

The production of these extra models must arouse today's collector's curiosity until they recall with the help of the recent Tutenkamen Exhibition at the British Museum that the discovery of the young King's Tomb in 1922 was only the climax of many years' aggressive investigation of the region of several teams of explorers. Indeed, from a commercial point of view, the Goss factory would have found it much more convenient had the tomb been discovered two or three years later as no sooner had the models made their appearance than interest in Egyptology began to wane.

The models "in preparation" were given numbers and why 2, 3, 12, 13, 14 and 15 were not used can only be a matter for speculation. The most probable explanation is that around twenty designs of suitable "pots" were prepared for the consideration of the Cairo Agent. He in turn selected the models thought to be most suitable and the rejected designs account for the missing numbers.

An Egyptian Lotus Vase was chosen in 1923 as the model for sale exclusively to members of the International League of Goss Collectors and at around the same time two further models were issued by the Goss factory and these together with the Wembley Lion were put on sale at the 1924 Exhibition.

Cairo or Alexandria may also be considered matching on any Egyptian piece.

EGYPTIAN WATER JAR

56mm   3.75   7.50

(Goss Record. 9th Edition: Page 37)
Matching Arms: EGYPT

EGYPTIAN CANOPIC JAR WITH ANUBIS HEAD No. 1

(Goss Record. 9th Edition: Page 37)   76mm   56.50   82.50
This most unusual model is marked 'copyright'. The anubis head is detachable and the model is incomplete without this lid, which is worth £27.50.
Matching Arms: EGYPT

EGYPTIAN KOHL POT No 4

66mm   21.75   35.00

(Goss Record. 9th Edition: Page 37)
This model is marked 'copyright'
Matching Arms: EGYPT

Dover Mortar

Durham Sanctuary Knocker Mug

Dutch Sabot

Eddystone Lighthouse

Egyptian Water Jar

Egyptian Canopic Jar with Anubis Head No. 1

Egyptian Kohl Pot No. 4

Egyptian Kohl Pot No. 5

Egyptian Kohl Pot No. 6

Egyptian Alabaster Vase No. 7

Egyptian Alabaster Vase No. 8

Egyptian Alabaster Bowl No. 9

Model			With any Arms £ p	With Matching Arms £ p
EGYPTIAN KOHL POT No 5 (Goss Record. 9th Edition: Page 37) This model is marked 'copyright' *Matching Arms: EGYPT*		60mm	10.50	35.00
EGYPTIAN KOHL POT No 6 (Goss Record. 9th Edition: Page 37) This model is marked 'copyright' *Matching Arms: EGYPT*	Dia.	70mm	12.50	35.00
EGYPTIAN ALABASTER VASE No 7 (Goss Record. 9th Edition: Page 37) This model is marked 'copyright' *Matching Arms: EGYPT*		105mm	16.00	35.00
EGYPTIAN ALABASTER VASE No 8 (Goss Record. 9th Edition: Page 37) This model is marked 'copyright' *Matching Arms: EGYPT*		105mm	16.00	35.00
EGYPTIAN ALABASTER BOWL No 9 (Goss Record. 9th Edition: Page 37) This model is marked 'copyright' *Matching Arms: EGYPT*		58mm	10.50	35.00
EGYPTIAN WOODEN EWER No 10 (Goss Record. 9th Edition: Page 37) This model is marked 'copyright' *Matching Arms: EGYPT*		66mm	12.50	35.00
EGYPTIAN PORCELAIN EWER No 11 (Goss Record. 9th Edition: Page 37) This model is marked 'copyright' *Matching Arms: EGYPT*		58mm	16.00	35.00
EGYPTIAN PORCELAIN BOTTLE No 16 (Goss Record. 9th Edition: Page 37) This model is marked 'copyright', and is the rarest of the Egyptian models. *Matching Arms: EGYPT*		68mm	35.00	65.00
EGYPTIAN LOTUS VASE International League model for 1923. *Correct Arms: THE INTERNATIONAL LEAGUE OF GOSS COLLECTORS*		80mm		130.00

Egyptian Wooden Ewer
No. 10

Egyptian Porcelain Ewer
No. 11

Egyptian Porcelain Bottle
No. 16

Egyptian Lotus Vase

Egyptian Mocha Cup
(Bowl Shaped)

Egyptian Mocha Cup
(Egg-cup Shaped)

Elizabethan Jug

Ellesmere Ancient British
Canoe

Eton Vase

Exeter Goblet

Exeter Vase

Felixstowe Roman Ewer

Model	With any Arms £ p	With Matching Arms £ p
EGYPTIAN MOCHA CUP (Bowl Shaped) Named 40mm	4.50	10.00
Matching Arms: EGYPT Un-named 40mm	3.00	7.50

This model is not listed in any edition of the Goss Record.
It is described as bowl shaped so as to distinguish it
from the Egg Cup shaped variety, also named Egyptian
Mocha Cup and bearing the same registration number
(572083). This piece always appears to be particularly
finely modelled, the porcelain being very thin and
delicate. It is found both named and un-named.

EGYPTIAN MOCHA CUP (Egg Cup Shaped) Named 52mm	4.75	11.75
Matching Arms: EGYPT Un-named 52mm	4.50	8.75

This model is not listed in any edition of the Goss
Record. It is described as Egg Cup shaped so as to
distinguish it from the Bowl shaped version, also
named Egyptian Mocha Cup and carrying the same
registration number (572083). It is found both named
and un-named.

for EGYPTIAN PYRAMID
see Great Pyramid

for ELIZABETHAN BUSHEL MEASURE
see Appleby Elizabethan Bushel Measure

ELIZABETHAN JUG	95mm	14.50	21.75

(Goss Record. 8th Edition: Page 43)
This model is listed 'Miscellaneous' in the Goss Record
under the heading at the end of the listing of special
historical shapes, that is, it was available to any agent
and did not have a "matching" or local coat of arms.
(Except possibly the arms of Queen Elizabeth, which
are priced here as matching). It is difficult to find this
model in fine condition as it was one of the first models
issued and the gilding and enamels of the coat of arms
are invariably worn. Indeed, few if any of this model
can have been manufactured after 1895 when the
newer models with specific local connections became
so much more popular. Frequently found impressed,
'W.H. GOSS' only, i.e. without the Gosshawk.

Model		With any Arms £ p	With Matching Arms £ p

ELLESMERE ANCIENT BRITISH CANOE
(Goss Record. 8th Edition: Page 31) (a) White glazed length 41.50 75.00
        (b) Brown† 149mm 215.00
This model is listed as bearing no arms in the 9th
Edition of the Goss Record. After 1921, a white glazed
version of this model must have been issued as it is
more commonly seen bearing a coat of arms.
Matching Arms: ELLESMERE

for ENGLISH WINE FLAGON
see London Christ's Hospital English Wine Flagon

ETON VASE   86mm 5.50 9.50
(Goss Record. 8th Edition: Page 16)
Matching Arms: FLOREAT ETONA (or WINDSOR)

EXETER GOBLET   130mm 10.00 14.50
(Goss Record. 8th Edition: Page 20)
Matching Arms: EXETER

EXETER VASE   63mm 3.50 6.50
(Goss Record. 8th Edition: Page 20) 101mm 7.00 11.00
Matching Arms: EXETER

for FARM LABOURER'S BOTTLE
see Luton Bottle

for FEEDING BOTTLE
See Wilderspool Roman Tetinae

FELIXSTOWE ROMAN EWER   73mm 4.50 8.75
(Goss Record. 8th Edition: Page 34) 114mm 10.00 14.50
Matching Arms: FELIXSTOWE

FELIXSTOWE ROMAN CINERARY URN 47mm 4.50 10.50
(Goss Record. 8th Edition: Page 34)
Matching Arms: FELIXSTOWE

FENNY STRATFORD POPPER   58mm 8.75 16.00
(Goss Record. 9th Edition: Page 11)
This model is marked 'copyright'
Matching Arms: FENNY STRATFORD

Model		With any Arms £ p	With Matching Arms £ p
FIMBER ANCIENT BRITISH CINERARY URN	106mm		130.00
International League Model for 1928.			
Correct Arms: THE INTERNATIONAL LEAGUE OF GOSS COLLECTORS			
for FISH BASKET			
see Alderney, Guernsey, Jersey or Sark Fish Basket			
(OLD) FLEMISH MELK POT	Max. Dia. 118mm	9.50	17.00
(Goss Record. 8th Edition: Page 42)			
The name of this model is spelt as above in the 8th Edition of the Goss Record (page 42) and on every model produced from the Goss factory and this being Flemish for milk is obviously correct. However, it is incorrectly spelt "milk" in the 9th Edition (page 37).			
Matching Arms: ANTWERPEN			
for FLOATING MINE			
see Contact Mine			
FOLKESTONE SALTWOOD ROMAN EWER	88mm	6.50	12.50
(Goss Record. 8th Edition: Page 27)			
Matching Arms: FOLKESTONE			
FOUNTAINS ABBEY, ABBOT'S CUP	44mm	3.75	11.00
(Goss Record. 8th Edition: Page 38)	76mm	8.75	16.00
also see Chapter headed 'POSTCARDS'			
Matching Arms: FOUNTAINS ABBEY			
FOUR SHIRE STONE	118mm	40.00	56.50
(Goss Record. 8th Edition: Page 31)			
This model has a delicate finial, which is particularly prone to damage.			
Matching Arms: CHIPPING NORTON			
FRASER CUACH	Length 104mm	8.25	17.50
(Goss Record. 9th Edition: Page 35)			
Matching Arms: FORT AUGUSTUS			
for FRID STOL			
see Hexham Abbey Frid Stol			

Felixstowe Roman Cinerary Urn

Fenny Stratford Popper

Fimber Ancient British Cinerary Urn

Flemish Melk Pot

Folkestone Roman Ewer

Fountains Abbey Cup

Four Shire Stone

Fraser Cuach

Froxfield Roman Bronze Drinking Bowl

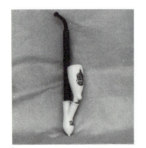

German Smoking Pipe

Gerrans Celtic Cinerary Urn

Glastonbury Jack

Model		With any Arms £ p	With Matching Arms £ p

FROXFIELD ROMAN BRONZE
DRINKING BOWL   Dia. 72mm   30.00   35.00
(Goss Record. 8th Edition: Page 36)
This model was originally sold without Arms, and subsequently with those of *MARLBOROUGH which are considered Matching.*

for GERMAN INCENDIARY BOMB
see Maldon (Essex) German Incendiary Bomb

GERMAN SMOKING PIPE   Overall   47.50
(Goss Record. 8th Edition: Page 45)   Length
Although manufactured as an ornamental object, it   252mm
is now thought by some to merit inclusion as an 'Historic
Object or Shape'.
It consists of a wooden stem and porcelain bowl and pipe.
It has no correct arms unless perhaps German

for GERMAN ZEPPELIN BOMB
see Bury St. Edmunds German Bomb

GERRANS CELTIC CINERARY URN
(Goss Record. 8th Edition: Page 18)

Matching Arms: FALMOUTH With 1 coat of arms	57mm	4.50	7.50
With 1 coat of arms	127mm	12.00	19.50
With 3 coats of arms	57mm	7.50	11.00
With 3 coats of arms	127mm	17.50	21.00

GIBRALTAR ALCARAZA or SPANISH CARAFE 68mm   4.00   15.25
(Goss Record. 8th Edition: Page 42)
This model can be found incorrectly labelled
'Gibraltar Carafe'.
Matching Arms: GIBRALTAR or SPAIN

Glastonbury collectors should see the marvellous two-page advertisement in the Goss Record. 8th Edition: Page 80–81.

GLASTONBURY (ABBOT BEERE'S) JACK   56mm   3.50   6.50
(Goss Record. 8th Edition: Page 32)
Matching Arms: GLASTONBURY

GLASTONBURY ANCIENT SALT CELLAR   82mm   10.50   16.50
(Goss Record. 8th Edition: Page 32)
Matching Arms: GLASTONBURY

Model		With any Arms £ p	With Matching Arms £ p
GLASTONBURY BRONZE BOWL	44mm	6.00	9.25
(Goss Record. 8th Edition: Page 31)	127mm	19.50	26.00
Matching Arms: GLASTONBURY			
The larger version can be found with or without three ball feet.			
GLASTONBURY ROMAN EWER	71mm	3.50	8.00
(Goss Record. 8th Edition: Page 32)			
Matching Arms: GLASTONBURY			
GLASTONBURY TERRA-COTTA BOWL	36mm	3.00	6.50
(Goss Record. 8th Edition: Page 31)			
Matching Arms: GLASTONBURY			
GLASTONBURY VASE (OR URN)	45mm	3.00	6.50
(Goss Record. 8th Edition: Page 31)			
Matching Arms: GLASTONBURY			

for GLEN DORGAL CINERARY URN
see Truro Glen Dorgal Cinerary Urn

GLOUCESTER JUG	44mm	3.50	8.25
(Goss Record. 8th Edition: Page 22)	95mm	10.00	17.00
Matching Arms: GLOUCESTER			
GNOSSUS ASHMOLEAN VASE	60mm		43.50
(Goss Record. 9th Edition: Pages 22, 41 and Plate C)			
International League Model for 1920.			
Correct Arms: THE INTERNATIONAL LEAGUE OF GOSS COLLECTORS			
GODALMING ANCIENT EWER	55mm	5.50	11.00
(Goss Record. 8th Edition: Page 34)			
Matching Arms: GODALMING			

for GOGARTH ANCIENT VASE
see (Gogarth) Llandudno Ancient Vase

GOODWIN SANDS CARAFE	61mm	3.50	5.00
(Goss Record. 8th Edition: Page 27)			
Acceptable Matching Arms: RAMSGATE, DEAL or WALMER			
GRAVESEND ORIENTAL WATER-COOLER	72mm	12.00	17.00
This model is marked 'copyright'			
Matching Arms: GRAVESEND			

Glastonbury Salt Cellar

Glastonbury Bronze Bowl

Glastonbury Roman Ewer

Glastonbury Terra-cotta Bowl

Glastonbury Vase

Gloucester Jug

Gnossus Ashmolean Vase

Godalming Ancient Ewer

Gibraltar Alcaraza

Gravesend Oriental Water Cooler

Goodwin Sands Carafe

Greek Amphora Vase

67

Great Pyramid

Greenwich Vase

Grinlow Tower

Guernsey Fish Basket

Guernsey Milk Can and Lid

Guildford Roman Vase

Guillemot Egg, open and closed

Guy's Porridge Pot

Guy's Porridge Pot (identical to Irish Bronze Pot)

Hammoga Amaui, Tonga

Hafod Vase and Lid

Hambledon Cricket Stone

Model		With any Arms £ p	With Matching Arms £ p
(THE) GREAT PYRAMID		35.00	65.00

(Goss Record. 8th Edition: Page 42)
Could be considered as a Monument or Building – often
appears chipped at the corners.
Matching Arms: EGYPT

GREEK AMPHORA VASE	138mm		43.50

(Goss Record. 9th Edition: Page 40 and Plate A)
International League Model for 1921.
*Correct Arms: THE INTERNATIONAL LEAGUE OF
GOSS COLLECTORS*

GREENWICH VASE	86mm	30.00	42.50

This model, which is extremely rare, is exactly the same
as the Eton Vase (and says so on its base).
Matching Arms: GREENWICH

GRINLOW TOWER	95mm	157.50	260.00

Probably the rarest white glazed Tower.
Matching Arms: BUXTON

GUERNSEY FISH BASKET	45mm	10.00	15.25
(Goss Record. 8th Edition: Page 17)	58mm	12.50	21.75

Matching Arms: GUERNSEY

GUERNSEY MILK CAN (and lid)	70mm		12.50
This model is incomplete without	108mm	11.75	16.50
its lid, value £7.00	140mm	14.50	19.50

(Goss Record. 9th Edition: Page 11)
Matching Arms: GUERNSEY

GUILDFORD ROMAN VASE	63mm	6.50	11.00

(Goss Record. 8th Edition: Page 34)
Matching Arms: GUILDFORD

GUILLEMOT EGG (See also BIRD'S EGG) (a) Closed	93mm	43.50	
Found closed, or open as hanging posy vase (b) Open	83mm	43.50	

either with or without arms, none of which may
be considered matching. It is however
preferable to have the arms of a coastal town
where such birds are found.

GUY'S PORRIDGE POT	50mm	4.00	11.00

(Goss Record. 8th Edition: Page 35)
Matching Arms: WARWICK

Hamworthy Lamp

Harrogate Ewer

Hastings Kettle

Hawes Ancient British Urn

Hawkins Henley Sculls in Presentation Box

Hereford Terracotta Kettle and Lid

Herne Bay Reculver Towers

Herne Bay Ancient Ewer

Hertford Ancient Ewer

Hexham Abbey Frid Stol

Hitchin Posset Cup

Hornsea Atwick Roman Vase

Model			With any Arms £ p	With Matching Arms £ p
GUY'S PORRIDGE POT		40mm		43.50

Better known as a small Irish Bronze Pot but named in large Gothic script on side. Only one example has been seen with the arms of Stratford-On-Avon.

HAAMOGA AMAUI, TONGA		82mm		850.00

The model is marked 'copyright'.

HAFOD VASE (and lid)		82mm	47.50	75.00

This model is marked 'copyright'. The lid has a knob on top which tends to get chipped. Can be found also with a sepia transfer of Devil's Bridge – the matching arms value of which is given here as there are no correct arms.

HAMBLEDON CRICKET STONE	Grey	80mm†	875.00	

(Goss Record. 9th Edition: Page 16)

HAMWORTHY LAMP		Length 100mm	7.00	12.50

(Goss Record. 8th Edition: Page 21)
Matching Arms: POOLE

HARROGATE ANCIENT EWER		62mm	3.50	7.50

(Goss Record. 8th Edition: Page 38)
Matching Arms: HARROGATE

HASTINGS KETTLE		51mm	3.25	6.50

(Goss Record. 8th Edition: Page 34)
Matching Arms: HASTINGS

HAWES ANCIENT BRITISH URN	Dia.	95mm	9.00	15.00

(Goss Record. 8th Edition: Page 38)
Matching Arms: HAWES

HAWKINS' HENLEY SCULL		Length 152mm		52.00

(Goss Record. 9th Edition: Page 25)

These sculls have never been seen other than with the (two) Henley Coats-of-Arms. The local agent had 'presentation' boxes made to sell them in pairs.
*Matching Arms: HENLEY ANCIENT or HENLEY-ON-
    THAMES*

for HEN CLOUD LEEK URN
see Leek Urn

Model			With any Arms £ p	With Matching Arms £ p
for HENLEY HAWKINS' SCULL see Hawkins' Henley Scull				
HEREFORD TERRA-COTTA KETTLE (and lid)		70mm	12.50	19.50
(Goss Record. 8th Edition: Page 24 and advertisement		121mm	19.50	30.00
page 66) *Matching Arms: HEREFORD*				
HERNE BAY RECULVER TOWERS (Goss Record. 8th Edition: Page 27)				
Matching Arms: HERNE BAY	(a) White glazed	101mm	80.00	125.00
	(b) Grey†	101mm	175.00	
	(c) Brown†	101mm	195.00	
HERNE BAY ANCIENT EWER		78mm	3.50	8.50
(Goss Record. 8th Edition: Page 27) *Matching Arms: HERNE BAY*				
HERTFORD ANCIENT EWER		69mm	5.50	11.00
(Goss Record. 8th Edition: Page 24) *Matching Arms: HERTFORD*				
HEXHAM ABBEY FRID STOL	(a) White unglazed	60mm	24.50	30.00
(Goss Record. 8th Edition: Page 30)	(b) White glazed	60mm	21.75	28.00
	(c) Brown	60mm	35.00	40.00
	(d) Brown, Two piece as pin box	60mm		
	and lid		85.00	85.00

Each of the three basic versions of this model can
be found both with and without a coat of arms, and
occasionally in the original box in which they were
sold. A different two-piece version has only recently
come to light.
Matching Arms: HEXHAM ABBEY

Model	With any Arms £ p	With Matching Arms £ p
for HIGHLAND CUACH or WHISKEY CUP see National Highland Cuach or Whisky Cup		
for HIGHLAND MILK CROGAN see Stornaway Highland Milk Crogan		
HITCHIN POSSET CUP	4.50	8.25

HITCHIN POSSET CUP — 51mm

(Goss Record. 8th Edition: Page 24)
Matching Arms: HITCHIN

Model		With any Arms £ p	With Matching Arms £ p
HORNSEA ATWICK ROMAN VASE (Goss Record. 8th Edition: Page 38) *Matching Arms: HORNSEA*	51mm	4.50	7.50
(THE OLD) HORSE SHOE (Goss Record. 8th Edition: Page 43) This model is classified under the heading 'Miscellaneous' at the end of the special historical shapes list in the 9th Edition of the Goss Record. If the decoration is large, then the descriptive matter is printed on the reverse. *It has no matching arms*	115mm	13.00	
HORSHAM JUG (Goss Record. 8th Edition: Page 34) *Matching Arms: HORSHAM*	60mm	3.25	8.25
HUNSTANTON EWER (Goss Record. 8th Edition: Page 29) *Matchin Arms: HUNSTANTON*	65mm	3.50	8.25
HYTHE CROMWELLIAN MORTAR (Goss Record. 8th Edition: Page 27) *Matching Arms: HYTHE*	38mm	5.50	9.25
HYTHE CRYPT SKULL (Goss Record. 9th Edition: Page 20)			
(a) Small pale yellow†	38mm	30.00	
(b) Large white†	72mm	95.00	
(c) Large pale yellow†	72mm	117.50	
ILKLEY ROMAN EWER (Goss Record. 8th Edition: Page 38) *Matching Arms: ILKLEY*	60mm 132mm	3.00 11.75	4.75 24.50
IPSWICH ANCIENT EWER (Goss Record. 8th Edition: Page 34) *Matching Arms: IPSWICH*	60mm	4.75	8.25
IPSWICH ROMAN EWER (Goss Record. 8th Edition: Page 34) *Matching Arms: IPSWICH*	98mm	11.75	17.50
IRISH BRONZE POT (Goss Record. 8th Edition: Page 40) *Matching Arms: IRELAND*	43mm 72mm	3.00 7.00	7.00 11.00

73

(The Old) Horse Shoe

Horsham Jug

Hunstanton Ewer

Hythe Cromwellian Mortar

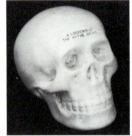
Hythe Crypt Skull

Ilkley Roman Ewer

Ipswich Ancient Ewer

Ipswich Roman Ewer

Irish Bronze Pot

Ancient Irish Cruisken

Irish Mather

Irish Wooden Noggin

Model		With any Arms £ p	With Matching Arms £ p
(ANCIENT) IRISH CRUISKEN International League Model for 1929 *Correct Arms: THE INTERNATIONAL LEAGUE OF GOSS COLLECTORS*	95mm		130.00
IRISH MATHER (Goss Record. 8th Edition: Page 40 and advertise- ment page 61) also see chapter headed 'POSTCARDS' *Matching Arms: IRELAND* *The large size is usually multi-crested and carries a verse.*	76mm 152mm	5.25 30.00	11.00 47.50
IRISH WOODEN NOGGIN (Goss Record. 8th Edition: Page 40) *Matching Arms: IRELAND*	63mm	5.25	11.00
for ISLE OF WIGHT ROMAN EWER see Brading Ewer			
for ITALIAN EWER see Pompeian Ewer			
ITALIAN KRATER International League Model for 1922. *Correct Arms: THE INTERNATIONAL LEAGUE OF GOSS COLLECTORS*	100mm		60.00
ITFORD URN (Goss Record. 8th Edition: Page 35) *Matching Arms: LEWES*	66mm 111mm	4.50 13.00	11.00 24.50
JAPAN EWER (Goss Record. 8th Edition: Page 42) Both sizes are found named and un-named. Same price. *Matching Arms: JAPAN*	90mm 200mm	7.50 19.50	15.25 24.50
JERSEY FISH BASKET (Goss Record. 8th Edition: Page 17) This model can be found without a coat of arms but this has little or no bearing on the catalogue price. *Matching Arms: JERSEY*	45mm 58mm	7.50 10.00	12.50 16.00

Italian Krater

Itford Urn

Japan Ewer

Jersey Fish Basket

Jersey Milk Can and Lid

Kettering Urn

King Richard's Well Cover

Kendal Jug

Kininmonth Moss Pot

*King's Newton Anglo-Saxon
Cinerary Urn*

Lancashire Clog

Lancaster Jug

Model		With any Arms £ p	With Matching Arms £ p
JERSEY MILK CAN AND LID	70mm		12.50
(Goss Record. 9th Edition: Page 11)	108mm	10.50	17.00
This model is incomplete without	140mm	12.50	19.50
its lid which is worth £7.00			
Matching Arms: JERSEY			

for JOHN BARROW'S MONUMENT
see Sir John Barrow's Monument, Ulverston

Model		With any Arms	With Matching Arms
KENDAL JUG	86mm	4.50	11.00
(Goss Record. 8th Edition: Page 36)	145 mm	17.50	24.50
Matching Arms: KENDAL			
KETTERING URN			
(Goss Record. 8th Edition: Page 30)	43mm	3.25	9.25
Matching Arms: KETTERING			
KING RICHARD'S WELL COVER	100mm	157.50	215.00
(Goss Record. 9th Edition: Page 21)			
Matching Arms: MARKET BOSWORTH			
KING'S NEWTON ANGLO-SAXON			
CINERARY URN	(a) 60mm		26.00
(Goss Record. 9th Edition: Pages 22, 41 and	(b) 60mm		35.00
Plate B)			
This model was first introduced bearing the			
League of Goss Collectors Motif (a) and			
re-introduced later bearing the International			
League of Goss Collectors Motif (b).			
KININMONTH MOSS ANCIENT POT	49mm	8.75	24.50
(Goss Record. 9th Edition: Page 35 and Plate M)			
This model is marked 'copyright'			
Matching Arms: OLD DEER			

for KIRKPARK URN
see Musselburgh Urn

Model		With any Arms	With Matching Arms
LANCASHIRE CLOG	Length	30.00	41.50
(Goss Record. 9th Edition: Page 21)	93mm		
This model is marked 'copyright'			
Matching Arms: LANCASHIRE			
LANCASTER JUG	68mm	3.50	7.50
(Goss Record. 8th Edition: Page 27)			
Matching Arms: LANCASTER			

Lanlawren Celtic Sepulchral Urn

Largs Memorial Tower

Las Palmas Ancient Covered Jarra and Lid

Las Palmas Ancient Earthen Jar

Las Palmas Ancient Jarra

Laxey Urn

Leek Urn

Leicester Tyg

Leiston Abbey Pitcher

Letchworth Celtic Cinerary Urn

Letchworth Carinated Roman Vase

Lewes Vase

Model		With any Arms £ p	With Matching Arms £ p

for LANDGATE CANNON BALL
see Rye Cannon Ball

LANLAWREN CELTIC SEPULCHRAL URN   50mm   3.25   7.00
(Goss Record. 8th Edition: Page 18)   102mm   11.75   20.00
There are no correct arms for this model but any Cornish arms would be considered as local. Lanlawren is part of Falmouth and this must therefore be considered the 'correct' arms although the Goss record does not give the Falmouth agency as being stockists of this model.

(BATTLE OF) LARGS MEMORIAL TOWER   128mm   26.00   40.00
(Goss Record. 8th Edition: Page 40)
Matching Arms: LARGS

LAS PALMAS ANCIENT COVERED JARRA   58mm   7.50   17.50
(Goss Record. 8th Edition: Page 42)
This model is incomplete without its lid, value £5.00
Matching arms: LAS PALMAS

LAS PALMAS ANCIENT EARTHEN JAR   58mm   4.75   17.50
(Goss Record. 8th Edition: Page 42)
Matching Arms: LAS PALMAS

LAS PALMAS ANCIENT JARRA   53mm   6.00   16.00
(Goss Record. 8th Edition: Page 42)
Matching Arms: LAS PALMAS

for LAS PALMAS CANARY PORRON
see Canary Porron

LAXEY URN   Dia.   55mm   5.25   11.00
(Goss Record. 9th Edition: Page 19)
This model can be found bearing arms on the base (on the inside) or in the usual position on the outside.
Matching Arms: LAXEY, ISLE OF MAN

for LEEK
see Welsh Leek

LEEK URN   63mm   4.75   11.00
(Goss Record. 8th Edition: Page 32)
Matching Arms: LEEK

Model			With any Arms £ p	With Matching Arms £ p
LEICESTER TYG	(a) with 1 coat of arms	59mm	6.50	11.00
(Goss Record. 8th Edn: Page 28) (b) with 3 coats of arms		59mm	7.50	13.50
Matching Arms: LEICESTER				
LEISTON ABBEY PITCHER		61mm	3.50	12.50
(Goss Record. 8th Edition: Page 34)		107mm	11.00	19.50
Matching Arms: LEISTON ABBEY				
LETCHWORTH CELTIC CINERARY URN		97mm	23.00	30.00
(Goss Record. 9th Edition: Page 19 and Plate J)				
This model is marked 'copyright'				
Matching Arms: LETCHWORTH				
LETCHWORTH CARINATED ROMAN VASE		60mm	52.50	105.00
This model is marked 'copyright'				
Matching Arms: LETCHWORTH				
LEWES ROMAN VASE		35mm	3.00	7.50
(Goss Record. 8th Edition: Page 35)				
Matching Arms: LEWES				

for LEWES URN
see Itford Urn

for LHANNAN SHEE CUP
see Ballafletcher (Cup of)

Model		With any Arms £ p	With Matching Arms £ p
LICHFIELD JUG	57mm	3.25	11.00
(Goss Record. 8th Edition: Page 32)	121mm	12.50	19.50
Matching Arms: LICHFIELD			

LINCOLN LEATHER JACK
(Goss Record. 8th Edition: Page 28)

		With any Arms £ p	With Matching Arms £ p
(a)	56mm	3.50	7.00
(b) Correct marking – coloured bell and shield, no arms	56mm		30.00
(c)	153mm	15.25	21.75
(d) Matt black with multi-coloured bells, no arms	153mm		870.00

Matching Arms: LINCOLN

Model		With any Arms £ p	With Matching Arms £ p
LINCOLN VASE	57mm	4.00	7.50
(Goss Record. 8th Edition: Page 28)	88mm	7.50	10.00
Matching Arms: LINCOLN			
LITTLEHAMPTON ROMAN EWER	73mm	4.50	8.25
(Goss Record. 8th Edition: Page 35)			
Matching Arms: LITTLEHAMPTON			

Lichfield Jug

Lincoln Leather Jack, small with City Ringers Decoration

Black Lincoln Leather Jack, large

Lincoln Vase

Littlehampton Roman Ewer

Llandudno (Little Orme) Roman Vase

Llandudno (Gogarth) Ancient Vase

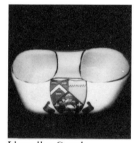

Llangollen Coracle

Lobster Trap

London Christ's Hospital English Wine Flagon

London Stone

Longships Lighthouse

81

Model		With any Arms £ p	With Matching Arms £ p
LLANDUDNO (LITTLE ORME) ROMAN VASE (Goss Record. 9th Edition: Page 34 and Plate K) This model is marked 'copyright' *Matching Arms: LLANDUDNO*	82mm	9.25	15.25
LLANDUDNO (GOGARTH) ANCIENT VASE (Goss Record. 9th Edition: Pate 34 and Plate K) This model is marked 'copyright' *Matching Arms: LLANDUDNO*	84mm	8.25	15.25
LLANGOLLEN CORACLE (Goss Record. 8th Edition: Page 39) *Matching Arms: LLANGOLLEN* Usually found inscribed 'Welsh Coracle'	Length 77mm	13.00	21.00
LOBSTER TRAP (Goss Record. 8th Edition: Page 17) *Matching Arms: ANY OF THE CHANNEL ISLANDS*	51mm 84mm	8.75 15.25	11.75 19.50
LONDON CHRIST'S HOSPITAL ENGLISH WINE FLAGON (Goss Record. 8th Edition: Page 29) *Matching Arms: CHRIST'S HOSPITAL*	90mm	7.50	12.50
LONDON STONE (a) White† (Goss Record. 9th Edition: Page 22) (b) Brown†	109mm 109mm	82.50 130.00	
LONGSHIPS LIGHTHOUSE, LAND'S END (Goss Record. 8th Edition: Page 18) *Matching Arms: LAND'S END*	122mm	23.00	30.00
LOOE EWER (Goss Record. 8th Edition: Page 18) *Matching Arms: LOOE*	65mm	3.50	7.00
for LOTUS VASE see Egyptian Lotus Vase			
LOUTH ANCIENT EWER (Goss Record. 8th Edition: Page 28) *Matching Arms: LOUTH*	43mm 113mm	3.50 14.50	8.25 19.50
LUDLOW SACK BOTTLE (Goss Record. 8th Edition: Page 31) *Matching Arms: LUDLOW*	75mm	7.50	11.75

Model		With any Arms £ p	With Matching Arms £ p
LUTON BOTTLE OR COSTREL (Goss Record. 8th Edition: Page 16) *Matching Arms: LUTON*	Length 65mm	8.75	16.00
for LUTON COSTREL see Luton Bottle or Costrel			
LYME REGIS AMMONITE (Goss Record. 9th Edition: Page 14) *Matching Arms: LYME REGIS*	73mm	17.50	25.75
MADEIRA BULLOCK CAR This model is marked 'copyright' *Matching Arms: FUNCHAL, MADEIRA*	55mm		600.00
MAIDSTONE ROMAN EWER (Goss Record. 8th Edition: Page 27) *Matching Arms: MAIDSTONE*	82mm 130mm	4.75 9.00	9.00 16.00
MALDON (ESSEX) GERMAN INCENDIARY BOMB (Goss Record. 9th Edition: Page 16) This model is marked 'copyright'. It has a delicate handle which is frequently found broken. The model is of little value in this condition. *Matching Arms: MALDON*	75mm	18.50	24.50
Either MALTA or VALLETTA would be considered matching on any Maltese Model			
MALTESE CARAFFE (Goss Record. 8th Edition: Page 42) *Matching Arms: MALTA*	105mm	10.50	16.00
MALTESE DOUBLE-MOUTHED VASE (Goss Record. 9th Edition: Page 36 and Plate P) *Matching Arms: MALTA*	60mm	15.50	24.50
MALTESE FIRE GRATE (Goss Record. 8th Edition: Page 42) *Matching Arms: MALTA*	53mm	10.00	16.00
MALTESE FUNEREAL URN (Goss Record. 8th Edition: Page 42) *Matching Arms: MALTA*	61mm	4.50	11.00

Looe Ewer

Louth Ancient Ewer

Ludlow Sack Bottle

Luton Costrel

Lyme Regis Ammonite

Madeira Bullock Car

Maidstone Roman Ewer

Maldon Incendiary Bomb

Maltese Carafe

Maltese Double-mouthed Vase

Maltese Fire Grate

Maltese Funereal Urn

Model		With any Arms £ p	With Matching Arms £ p
MALTESE TWIN VASE (Goss Record. 9th Edition: Page 36 and Plate P) *Matching Arms: MALTA*	50mm	26.00	32.50
MALTESE TWO-WICK LAMP (Goss Record. 8th Edition: Page 42) *Matching Arms: MALTA*	Length 81mm	11.00	15.25
MALTESE VASE A CANARD (Goss Record. 9th Edition: Page 36) *Matching Arms: MALTA*	45mm	7.00	11.00
MANX LOBSTER POT This model is identical to the Lobster Trap. *Matching Arms: ISLE OF MAN*	Dia. 67mm		28.00
MANX PEEL POT (Goss Record. 8th Edition: Page 26) *Matching Arms: PEEL, ISLE OF MAN*	49mm	4.50	7.50
(ANCIENT) MANX SPIRIT MEASURE (Goss Record. 8th Edition: Page 26) *Matching Arms: PEEL, ISLE OF MAN*	68mm	5.25	8.75
(THE) MAPLE LEAF OF CANADA This model is marked 'copyright' and numbered 813. *Matching Arms: CANADA*	118mm	70.00	130.00
MARY, QUEEN OF SCOTS Face in high relief on (a) two-piece night-light (b) two or three-handled mug For illustration see page 160 *Correct Arms: MARY QUEEN OF SCOTS*	78mm 118mm	115.00 65.00	145.00 87.50
MELROSE CUP (Goss Record. 8th Edition: Page 40) Not really a model in the true sense of the word, it was designed by the Melrose Agent and first marketed exclusively by him. The bowl of the cup incorporates the same leaf design that can be found at the top of the pillars in Melrose Abbey. *Matching Arms: MELROSE ABBEY*	128mm	32.50	47.50

for MILK CROGAN
see Stornaway Highland Milk Crogan

Maltese Twin Vase

Maltese Two-wick Lamp

Maltese Vase à Canard

Manx Lobster Trap

Manx Peel Pot

Manx Spirit Measure

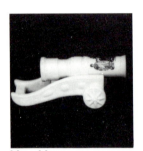

Mons Meg

The Maple Leaf of Canada

Melrose Cup

Minster Ancient Ewer

Minster Ancient Urn

Munich Beer Seidel

Model			With any Arms £ p	With Matching Arms £ p
MINSTER ANCIENT EWER		88mm	11.00	12.50
This model is marked 'copyright'				
Matching Arms: MINSTER				
MINSTER ANCIENT URN		65mm	7.50	12.50
This model is marked 'copyright'				
Matching Arms: MINSTER				

for MONMOUTH MASK
See Chapter headed PARIAN WARE (C)

for MONNOW GATE
see Old Gateway on Monnow Bridge

Model			With any Arms £ p	With Matching Arms £ p
MONS MEG, EDINBURGH CASTLE		Length	30.00	35.00
(Goss Record. 8th Edition: Page 40)		122mm		
Matching Arms: EDINBURGH				
MUNICH BEER SEIDEL		52mm	24.50	52.50
Matching Arks: MUNICH (MUNCHEN)				
MUSSELBURGH KIRKPARK ANCIENT URN		51mm	3.00	8.25
(Goss Record. 8th Edition: Page 40)				
Matching Arms: MUSSELBURGH				

for MYCENAEAN VASE
see Cyprus Mycenaean Vase

NATIONAL HIGHLAND CUACH or WHISKY CUP
(Goss Record. 8th Edition: Page 40)
Any 'Highland' Arms are considered matching.

			Width 94mm	5.25	10.50

NEWBURY LEATHER BOTTLE
(Goss Record. 8th Edition: Page 16)

Matching Arms: NEWBURY	(a)	58mm	3.50	7.50
	(b)	114mm	8.75	16.00
	(c) With Stopper	125mm	30.00	40.00

NEWCASTLE (STAFFORDSHIRE) CUP		70mm	8.75	14.50

(Goss Record. 8th Edition: Page 32)
Matching Arms: NEWCASTLE-UNDER-LYME

NEWCASTLE CASTLE	(a) White glazed	88mm	130.00	175.00
Matching Arms: NEWCASTLE	(b) Brown†	88mm	300.00	

Musselburgh or Kirkpark Urn

National Highland Cuach

Newbury Leather Bottle, small

Newbury Leather Bottle, (large) with Stopper

Newcastle (Staffordshire) Cup

Newcastle Castle

Newcastle Jug

North Foreland Lighthouse

Northwich Sepulchral Urn

Norwegian Bucket

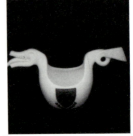

Norwegian Dragon-shaped Beer Bowl

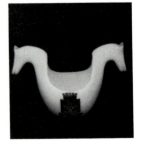

Norwegian Horse-shaped Beer Bowl

Model			With any Arms £ p	With Matching Arms £ p
NEWCASTLE JUG		63mm	3.25	8.25
(Goss Record. 8th Edition: Page 30)				
Matching Arms: NEWCASTLE				
for NORMAN TOWER, CHRISTCHURCH				
see Christchurch Priory Church Norman Tower				
NORTH FORELAND LIGHTHOUSE		108mm	35.00	46.50
(Goss Record. 8th Edition: Page 27)				
Matching Arms: BROADSTAIRS or RAMSGATE				
NORTHWICH SEPULCHRAL URN		85mm		195.00
International League Model for 1930.				
Correct Arms: THE INTERNATIONAL LEAGUE OF GOSS COLLECTORS				
NORWEGIAN BUCKET		58mm	8.75	35.00
(Goss Record. 8th Edition: Page 42)				
Matching Arms: NORWAY				
NORWEGIAN DRAGON-SHAPED BEER BOWL		Length 155mm	16.00	35.00
(Goss Record. 8th Edition: Page 42)				
Matching Arms: NORWAY				
NORWEGIAN HORSE-SHAPED BEER BOWL		Length 115mm	14.50	35.00
(Goss Record. 8th Edition: Page 42)				
Matching Arms: NORWAY				
NORWEGIAN WOODEN SHOE		Length 103mm	14.50	40.00
(Goss Record. 8th Edition: Page 42)				
Matching Arms: NORWAY				
NORWICH URN		51mm	3.25	6.50
(Goss Record. 8th Edition: Page 29)		62mm	4.50	8.25
Matching Arms: NORWICH		88mm	8.75	15.25
for NOSE OF BRASENOSE				
see (The Nose of) Brasenose				
NOTTINGHAM EWER	(a) 1 crest	63mm	3.50	7.50
(Goss Record. 8th Edition: Page 30)	(b) 2 crests	63mm	4.50	8.25
Matching Arms: NOTTINGHAM				

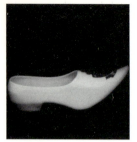

Norwegian Wooden Shoe

Norwich Urn

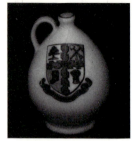

Nottingham Ewer

Nottingham Urn

Old Gateway on Monnow Bridge

Orkney Craisie

Ostend Flemish Bottle

Ostend Flemish Tobacco Jar

Ostend Vase

Oxford Ewer

Oxford Jug

Painswick Pot

Model			With any Arms £ p	With Matching Arms £ p
NOTTINGHAM URN (Goss Record. 8th Edition: Page 30 and advertisement page 79) *Matching Arms: NOTTINGHAM*		40mm	3.25	5.00

for OLD BRAZIER (SCILLY ISLES)
see Tresco Old Brazier

OLD GATEWAY ON MONNOW BRIDGE
(Goss Record. 9th Edition: Page 23 and Plate J)

	(a) White glazed	95mm	70.00	110.00
	(b) Brown†	95mm	215.00	

This model is the "MONNOW GATE" and not "MONMOW GATE" as mis-spelt in the 9th Edition of the Goss Record and on the model itself. The side gates are found both open and closed.
Matching Arms: MONMOUTH

for OLD HORSESHOE
see Horseshoe (The Old)

for OLD PILLION STONE, FLOWERGATE, WHITBY
see Whitby Pillion Stone

ORKNEY CRAISIE (Goss Record. 9th Edition: Page 35) This model has a high thin handle which can frequently be found cracked if not broken. *Matching Arms: ORKNEY*	80mm	16.00	24.50

OSTEND FLEMISH BOTTLE (Goss Record. 8th Edition: Page 42) *Matching Arms: OSTENDE*	65mm	4.75	12.50

OSTEND FLEMISH TOBACCO JAR (Goss Record. 8th Edition: Page 42) *Matching Arms: OSTENDE*	54mm	3.25	10.50

OSTEND VASE (Goss Record. 8th Edition: Page 42) *Matching Arms: OSTENDE*	57mm	3.25	11.00

OXFORD EWER (Goss Record. 8th Edition: Page 31) *Matching Arms: OXFORD*	76mm 126mm	4.00 9.25	8.25 12.50

Model			With any Arms £ p	With Matching Arms £ p
OXFORD JUG (Goss Record. 8th Edition: Page 31) *Matching Arms: OXFORD*		173mm	15.25	24.75
PAINSWICK POT (Goss Record. 8th Edition: Page 22) *Matching Arms: PAINSWICK*		50mm	3.00	11.00
PANAMA VASE *Matching Arms: PANAMA*		128mm	24.75	43.50
PENMAENMAWR URN (Goss Record. 8th Edition: Page 39) *Matching Arms: PENMAENMAWR*		45mm	3.25	10.50
for PERTH CORONATION CHAIR see Coronation Chair, Perth				
PETERBOROUGH TRIPOD (Goss Record. 8th Edition: Page 30) *Matching Arms: PETERBOROUGH*		47mm	7.00	11.00
for PILGRIM'S BOTTLE see Ancient Costril				
for PINE CONE see Bournemouth Pine Cone				
for PIPE see German Smoking Pipe				
PLYMOUTH JUG (Goss Record. 8th Edition: Page 20) *Matching Arms: PLYMOUTH*		55mm	3.25	7.50
POMPEIAN EWER (Goss Record. 8th Edition: Page 42) Both sizes are also found un-named – Same price. *Any Italian arms could be considered matching*		91mm 208mm	5.25 16.00	19.50 35.00
for POPE'S PIPE, TWICKENHAM see Twickenham Antique Pipe				
PORTLAND LIGHTHOUSE (Goss Record. 8th Edition: Page 21) *Matching Arms: PORTLAND*	(a) Black band (b) Brown band (c) Orange band	120mm 120mm 120mm	52.00 32.50 95.00	70.00 52.50 130.00

Panama Vase

Penmaenmawr Urn

Perth Coronation Chair

Peterborough Tripod

Plymouth Jug

Pompeian Ewer

Portland Lighthouse

Portland Vase

Preston Bushel Measure

Queen Elizabeth's Riding Shoe

Queen Phillippa's Record Chest

Queen Victoria's First Shoe

Model				With any Arms £ p	With Matching Arms £ p
PORTLAND VASE	(a)	51mm		3.50	5.00
	(b)	51mm		21.75	30.00
	(c)	51mm			21.75

This is one of the most interesting models as some have commemorative wording on the base marking the anniversary of the death of Josiah Wedgwood (b) and are much sought-after. This variety is thought to have been part of a limited edition (possibly 1,000) and collectors picking up every Portland Vase could easily have a pleasant surprise. Mr. J.J. Jarvis, when starting the League of Goss Collectors, chose this as the first 'League' model (c).

Collectors may read about the discovery and history of the original in the Goss Record. 8th Edition: Page 28. There are no correct arms for this model as it is currently in the British Museum. As there are no recorded arms for Lord Portland, the author suggests that the City of London arms are the most appropriate.

(b) JOSIAH WEDGWOOD
Matching Arms for (b): JOSIAH WEDGWOOD

PRESTON OLD BUSHEL MEASURE	Dia.	58mm		56.50	110.00

(Goss Record. 9th Edition: Page 21 and Plate M)
This model is marked 'copyright'. It is the rarest of the "small" bushels.
Matching Arms: PRESTON

for PRINCESS VICTORIA'S FIRST SLIPPER
see Queen Victoria's First Shoe

for PYRAMID
see Great Pyramid (The)

for QUEEN CHARLOTTE'S KETTLE
see Windsor Kettle

QUEEN ELIZABETH'S RIDING SHOE		Length		80.00	100.00
		105mm			

(Goss Record, 9th Edition: Page 16 and Plate L)
On page 16 of the Goss Record it is referred to as a slipper and under Plate L as a shoe.
This model is by far the rarest shoe.
It is marked 'copyright'.
Matching Arms: THAXTED

QUEEN PHILIPPA'S RECORD CHEST					
(Goss Record, 9th Edition: Page 33)	Length (a)	80mm		24.50	30.00
Matching Arms: KNARESBOROUGH (ABBEY)	(b)	94mm		24.50	30.00

Model				With any Arms £ p	With Matching Arms £ p
QUEEN VICTORIA'S FIRST SHOE	(a) Without Arms	102mm		25.75†	
(Goss Record. 8th Edition: Page 20)	(b) Pre-1901	102mm		25.75	32.50
	(c) Post-1901	102mm		25.75	32.50

An advertising letter was issued with
this model and increases its value by £5.
Matching Arms: QUEEN VICTORIA or SIDMOUTH

Model	Size	With any Arms £ p	With Matching Arms £ p
RAMSEY CRONK AUST CINERARY URN	59mm	4.50	10.00

(Goss Record. 8th Edition: Page 26)
Matching Arms: RAMSAY, ISLE OF MAN

Model	Size	With any Arms £ p	With Matching Arms £ p
RAMSGATE ROMANO-BRITISH EWER	47mm	9.50	14.50

This model is marked 'copyright' and 794.
Matching Arms: RAMSGATE

Model	Size	With any Arms £ p	With Matching Arms £ p
RAMSGATE ROMANO-BRITISH JUG	70mm	11.00	14.50

This model is marked 'copyright' and 795.
Matching Arms: RAMSGATE

Model	Size	With any Arms £ p	With Matching Arms £ p
RAMSGATE URN	75mm	7.50	12.50

This model is marked 'copyright' and 787.
Matching Arms: RAMSGATE

Model	Size	With any Arms £ p	With Matching Arms £ p
RAYLEIGH ANCIENT COOKING POT	33mm	3.50	7.00

(Goss Record. 8th Edition: Page 22)
Matching Arms: RAYLEIGH

Model	Size	With any Arms £ p	With Matching Arms £ p
READING JUG	82mm	3.00	6.50
	140mm	8.25	11.75

(Goss Record. 8th Edition: Parge 16)
Matching Arms: READING

Model	Size	With any Arms £ p	With Matching Arms £ p
READING (SILCHESTER) URN	50mm	3.00	5.50

(Goss Record. 8th Edition: Page 16)
Matching Arms: READING

Model	Size	With any Arms £ p	With Matching Arms £ p
READING (SILCHESTER) VASE	50mm	3.00	5.50

(Goss Record. 8th Edition: Page 16)
Matching Arms: READING

for RECULVER TOWERS
see Herne Bay Reculver Towers

Model	Size	With any Arms £ p	With Matching Arms £ p
ROCHESTER BELLARMINE JUG	65mm	3.50	8.25

(Goss Record. 8th Edition: Page 27)
Matching Arms: ROCHESTER

Ramsey Cronk Aust Cinerary Urn

Ramsgate Romano-British Ewer

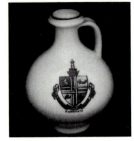

Ramsgate Romano-British Jug

Ramsgate Urn

Rayleigh Ancient Cooking Pot

Reading (Silchester) Urn

Reading (Silchester) Vase

Rochester Bellarmine Jug

Roman Mortarium

Roman Vase No. 783

Romsey Bushel

Rothesay Stone

Model			With any Arms £ p	With Matching Arms £ p
for ROMAN EWER see Cirencester Roman Ewer				
ROMAN MORTARIUM	(a) Named	Dia.	26.00	
(Goss Record. 8th Edition: Page 43)	(b) Un-named	95mm	11.00	
This model has no matching arms.				
for ROMAN TETINAE see Wilderspool Roman Tetinae				
ROMAN VASE	(a) White glazed	160mm	43.50	
This model is marked 'copyright' and 783.	(b) Lustre	160mm	40.00	
This model has no matching arms.				
ROMSEY BUSHEL	Dia.	68mm	8.00	15.25
(Goss Record. 8th Edition: Page 23) *Matching Arms: ROMSEY*				
ROTHESAY STONE	Brown†	Length	650.00	
(Goss Record. 9th Edition: Page 35 and Plate G)		95mm		
RUFUS STONE		94mm	8.75	14.50
(Goss Record. 8th Edition: Page 23 and advertisement page 64) *Matching Arms: KING WILLIAM RUFUS*				
RUSSIAN SHRAPNEL SHELL		110mm	12.50	30.00
(Goss Record. War Edition. Pages 5 [illustrated] and 7) *Matching Arms: RUSSIA or ANY MILITARY BADGE could add* *£10–£40*				
RYE CANNON BALL Multi-coloured				
(Goss Record. 8th Edition: Page 35)	(a) On plinth	106mm	75.00	115.00
	(b) Without	68mm	26.00	50.00
Matching Arms: RYE				
SAFFRON WALDEN COVERED URN (and lid)		70mm	11.75	19.50
(Goss Record. 8th Edition: Page 22)		121mm	16.00	26.00
This model has a lid that looks very like an Egyptian Mummy's Head without which it is incomplete, value £8.00 *Matching Arms: SAFFRON WALDEN*				
ST. ALBANS ANCIENT COOKING POT		58mm	5.25	10.00
(Goss Record. 8th Edition: Page 24) *Matching Arms: ST. ALBANS*				

Rufus Stone

Russian Shrapnel Shell

Rye Cannon Ball with Plinth

Rye Cannon Ball without Plinth

Saffron Walden Covered Urn and lid

St. Albans Ancient Cooking Pot

St. Mary's Lighthouse, Whitley Bay

St. Neots Ancient Urn

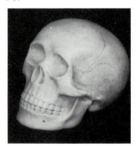

St. Simon of Sudbury's Skull

Salisbury Kettle

Salisbury Leather Jack

Salisbury Leather Gill

Model			With any Arms £ p	With Matching Arms £ p
ST. MARY'S LIGHTHOUSE, WHITLEY BAY		135mm	350.00	415.00

This model is not listed in any edition of the Goss Record
and is the rarest lighthouse.
Matching Arms: WHITLEY BAY

Model			With any Arms	With Matching Arms
ST. NEOTS ANCIENT URN		63mm	4.00	12.50

(Goss Record. 8th Edition: Page 24)
Matching Arms: ST. NEOTS

Model				
ST. SIMON OF SUDBURY'S SKULL				
	(a) White†	72mm	175.00	
	(b) Brown†	72mm	275.00	

Model		With any Arms	With Matching Arms
SALISBURY KETTLE	88mm	7.50	12.50
	133mm	11.75	16.00

(Goss Record. 8th Edition: Page 36)
Matching Arms: SALISBURY

Model		With any Arms	With Matching Arms
SALISBURY LEATHER JACK	44mm	3.50	7.50
	140mm	13.00	16.00

(Goss Record. 8th Edition: Page 36)
Matching Arms: SALISBURY

Model		With any Arms	With Matching Arms
SALISBURY LEATHER GILL	75mm	8.25	11.00

(Goss Record. 8th Edition: Page 36)
Matching Arms: SALISBURY

for SALTWOOD EWER
see Folkestone Roman Ewer

Model		With any Arms	With Matching Arms
SARK FISH BASKET	45mm		17.50
	58mm		22.50

(Goss Record. 8th Edition: Page 17)
Matching Arms: SARK (SERCQ)

Model		With any Arms	With Matching Arms
SARK MILK CAN (with lid)	70mm	17.50	26.00
	108mm		30.00
	140mm		35.00

(Goss Record. 9th Edition: Page 11)
This would be incomplete without its lid, value £7.00
Matching Arms: SARK (SERCQ)

Model		With any Arms	With Matching Arms
SCARBOROUGH JUG	51mm	4.00	7.50
	70mm	7.50	12.50

(Goss Record. 8th Edition: Page 38)
This model can be found wrongly labelled as a
'Scarborough Kettle'. Same price.
Matching Arms: SCARBOROUGH

Model		With any Arms £ p	With Matching Arms £ p
SCARBOROUGH KETTLE	66mm	7.50	12.50
(Goss Record. 8th Edition: Page 38)	88mm	12.50	21.75
This model can be found wrongly labelled as a 'Scarborough Jug', same price.			
Matching Arms: SCARBOROUGH			
SEAFORD URN	48mm	4.50	10.50
Early versions – 'Seaford Urn'			
(Goss Record. 8th Edition: Page 35)			
Matching Arms: SEAFORD			
SHAKESPEARE'S JUG	51mm	6.50	10.50
(Goss Record. 8th Edition: Page 35)	76mm	10.50	13.00
Matching Arms: WILLIAM SHAKESPEARE	88mm	15.25	19.50
for SHEPHERD'S CROWN SEA URCHIN			
see Steyning Shepherd's Crown			
SHREWSBURY EWER			
Early versions – 'The Uriconium Ewer'			
(Goss Record. 8th Edition: Page 31)	97mm	13.00	15.25
One of the first models to be introduced.			
Matching Arms: SHREWSBURY			
SHREWSBURY ROMANO-SALOPIAN EWER	68mm	4.00	7.50
(Goss Record. 8th Edition: Page 31)			
Matching Arms: SHREWSBURY			
for SILCHESTER URN			
see Reading (Silchester) Urn			
for SILCHESTER VASE			
see Reading (Silchester) Vase			
for SIMON OF SUDBURY'S SKULL			
see St. Simon of Sudbury's Skull			
SIR JOHN BARROW'S MONUMENT, ULVERSTON	120mm	65.00	87.00
Matching Arms: ULVERSTON			
SKEGNESS CLOCK TOWER	132mm	75.00	125.00
Matching Arms: SKEGNESS			

Sark Fish Basket

Sark Milk Can and Lid

Scarborough Jug

Scarborough Kettle

Seaford Urn

Shakespeare's Jug

*Shrewsbury 'Uriconium'
Ewer*

*Shrewsbury
Romano-Salopian Ewer*

*Sir John Barrow's
Monument, Ulverston*

Skegness Clock Tower

Southampton Ancient Pipkin

Southampton Bargate

Model		With any Arms £ p	With Matching Arms £ p
for SKULL			
see Hythe Crypt Skull			
or Yorick's Skull			
for SOLDIER'S WATER BOTTLE			
see Waterlooville Soldier's Water Bottle			
SOUTHAMPTON ANCIENT PIPKIN	56mm	3.25	7.50
(Goss Record. 8th Edition: Page 23)	76mm	11.00	16.00
Matching Arms: SOUTHAMPTON	101mm	11.00	19.50
SOUTHAMPTON BARGATE			
(Goss Record. 8th Edition: Page 23)			
(a) Small, white glazed	55mm	43.50	65.00
(b) Small, grey†	55mm	87.50	
(c) Large, white glazed or unglazed†	87mm	65.00	100.00
(d) Large, grey†	87mm	110.00	
(e) Large, brown†	87mm	175.00	
Matching Arms: SOUTHAMPTON			
SOUTHDOWN SHEEP BELL			
This model is identical to the Small	54mm	43.00	65.00
Swiss Cow Bell and is marked 'copyright'			
It has no correct arms – any Sussex downland arms			
are to be considered as matching			
SOUTHPORT VASE	50mm	3.50	8.25
(Goss Record. 8th Edition: Page 27)			
Matching Arms: SOUTHPORT			
SOUTHWOLD ANCIENT GUN	Length 94mm	157.50	260.00
(Goss Record. 9th Edition: Page 28)			
Matching Arms: SOUTHWOLD			
SOUTHWOLD JAR	88mm	3.00	8.25
(Goss Record. 8th Edition: Page 34)	140mm	12.50	13.50
Matching Arms: SOUTHWOLD			
for SPANISH CARAFE			
see Gibraltar Alcaraza			
STAFFORDSHIRE DRINKING CUP	111mm		60.00
International League Model for 1926.			
Correct Arms: THE INTERNATIONAL LEAGUE OF			
GOSS COLLECTORS			

Southport Vase

Southwold Ancient Gun

Southwold Jar

Staffordshire Drinking Cup

Staffordshire One-handled Tyg

Staffordshire Two-handled Tyg

Southdown Sheep Bell

Staffordshire Tyg

Steyning Sea Urchin

Stirling Pint Measure

Stockport Plague Stone

Stockton Salt Pot

Model			With any Arms £ p	With Matching Arms £ p
(STAFFORDSHIRE) ONE-HANDLED TYG (Goss Record. 8th Edition: Page 32) *Matching Arms: STAFFORDSHIRE*		65mm	3.50	6.50
(STAFFORDSHIRE) TWO-HANDLED TYG (Goss Record. 8th Edition: Page 32) *Matching Arms: STAFFORDSHIRE*		65mm	3.50	6.50
STAFFORDSHIRE TYG (Goss Record. 9th Edition: Pages 22 and 28 and Plate B) This model was first introduced bearing the League of Goss Collectors Motif (a) and re-introduced later bearing the International League of Goss Collectors Motif (b).	(a) (b)	70mm 70mm		35.00 43.50
STEYNING SHEPHERD'S CROWN SEA URCHIN (Goss Record. 9th Edition: Page 29) This model is marked 'copyright'. *Matching Arms: STEYNING*		50mm	17.50	26.00
STIRLING PINT MEASURE (Goss Record. 8th Edition: Page 40) *Matching Arms: STIRLING*		61mm	6.50	11.00
STOCKPORT PLAGUE STONE (Goss Record. 8th Edition: Page 17) *Matching Arms: STOCKPORT*		Length 75mm	12.50	15.25
STOCKTON ANCIENT SALT POT (Goss Record. 8th Edition: Page 21) *Matching Arms: STOCKTON-ON-TEES*		73mm	4.50	10.50
STORNAWAY HIGHLAND MILK CROGAN (Goss Record. 8th Edition: Page 40) *Matching Arms: STORNAWAY*		56mm	4.50	13.00
STRATFORD-ON-AVON SANCTUARY KNOCKER in high relief on two-handled mug (Goss Record. 9th Edition: page 30) This Model is marked 'copyright' *Matching Arms: STRATFORD-ON-AVON*		Height of detail 62mm	145.00	225.00
STRATFORD-ON-AVON TOBY BASIN Multi-coloured (Goss Record. 8th Edition: Page 35)		53mm	65.00†	

Stornaway Highland Milk Crogan

Stratford-on-Avon Sanctuary Knocker

Startford-on-Avon Toby Basin

Stratford-on-Avon Toby Jug

Sunderland Bottle

Swindon Vase

Swiss Cow Bell

Swiss Milk Bucket

Swiss Milk Pot and lid

Swiss Vinegar Bottle

Teignmouth Lighthouse

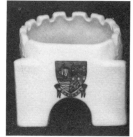

Tenby Gateway

Model			With any Arms £ p	With Matching Arms £ p
STRATFORD-ON-AVON TOBY JUG **Multi-coloured** (Goss Record. 8th Edition: Page 35)		78mm	40.00†	
SUNDERLAND BOTTLE (Goss Record. 8th Edition: Page 21 and advertisement page 65) *Matching Arms: SUNDERLAND*		58mm	3.25	7.00
SWINDON VASE (Goss Record. 8th Edition: page 36) *Matching Arms: SWINDON*		55mm 110mm	3.25 8.00	6.50 10.00
SWISS COW BELL (Goss Record. 8th Edition: Page 43) Only the 76mm size listed in the Goss Record. *Matching Arms: SWITZERLAND or any arms in that country*		51mm 76mm	7.50 8.25	13.00 21.00
SWISS MILK BUCKET (Goss Record. 8th Edition: Page 43) *Matching Arms: SWITZERLAND or any arms in that country*		56mm 82mm	6.00 8.00	30.00 30.00
SWISS MILK POT (and lid) (Goss Record. 8th Edition: Page 43) Often found cracked in the base This model is incomplete without its lid which is valued at£7.00 *Matching Arms: SWITZERLAND or any Arms in that country*		82mm	11.00	22.50
SWISS VINEGAR BOTTLE (Goss Record. 8th Edition: Page 43) *Matching Arms: SWITZERLAND or any Arms in that country*		Length 75mm	6.00	19.50
TEIGNMOUTH LIGHTHOUSE (Goss Record. 8th Edition: Page 20) *Matching Arms: TEIGNMOUTH*		115mm	30.00	40.00
TENBY GATEWAY *Matching Arms: TENBY*	(a) White glazed (b) Brown	65mm 65mm	87.50 275.00	145.00 275.00
TEWKESBURY URN (Goss Record. 8th Edition: Page 22) *Matching Arms: TEWKESBURY*		45mm	3.25	7.00
TINTERN ANCIENT WATER BOTTLE (Goss Record. 8th Edition: Page 29) *Matching Arms: TINTERN ABBEY*		76mm	5.25	8.25

Model		With any Arms £ p	With Matching Arms £ p

for TOBY BASIN
see Stratford-on-Avon Toby Basin

for TOBY JUG
see Stratford-on-Avon Toby Jug

TONBRIDGE EASTCHEAP ROMAN EWER   63mm   3.50   8.25
(Goss Record. 8th Edition: Page 27)
Matching Arms: TONBRIDGE

TRESCO OLD BRAZIER   69mm   11.00   15.25
(Goss Record. 8th Edition: Page 18)
Matching Arms: SCILLY ISLES (DORRIEN-SMITH)

TRESVANNACK ANCIENT URN   55mm   5.25   7.00
(Goss Record. 8th Edition: Page 18)
Matching Arms: PENZANCE (PENSANS A.D.)

TRURO GLEN DORGAL CINERARY URN   54mm   4.00   7.00
(Goss Record. 8th Edition: Page 18)
Matching Arms: TRURO

TUSCAN VASE   (a) White glazed 150mm   110.00
This model is marked 'copyright 785' (b) Lustre   150mm   85.00
It has no correct matching arms

TWICKENHAM ANTIQUE POPE'S PIPE   Length
(Goss Record. 8th Edition: Page 29)   118mm   32.50   42.50
Matching Arms: TWICKENHAM

for TYG (ONE HANDLE)
see Staffordshire One-Handled Tyg

for TYG (TWO HANDLES)
see Staffordshire Two-Handled Tyg

**for ULVERSTON, SIR JOHN BARROW'S
    MONUMENT**
see Sir John Barrow's Monument, Ulverston

for URICONIUM EWER (early models so marked)
see Shrewsbury Ewer

for WALDEN ABBEY COVERED URN
see Saffron Walden Covered Urn

Tewkesbury Urn   *Tintern Water Bottle*   *Tonbridge Eastcheap Ewer*

Tresco Old Brazier   *Tresvannack Ancient Urn*   *Tuscan Vase*

Truro Glen Dorgal Cinerary Urn   *Twickenham Pope's Pipe*   *Walmer Roman Vase*

Wareham Bottle   *Waterlooville Bottle*   *Welsh Crochon*

Welsh Fish Basket

Welsh Hat

Welsh Jack and Lid

Welsh Leek

Welsh Milk Can and Lid

Welsh Picyn

Wensleydale Leather Jack

*Westminster Abbey
Coronation Chair*

Weymouth Roman Vase

Whitby Ammonite

Whitby Pillion Stone

Whitstable Roman Patera

Model			With any Arms £ p	With Matching Arms £ p
WALMER ROMAN VASE (Goss Record. 8th Edition: Page 27) *Matching Arms: WALMER or DEAL*		65mm	3.25	7.50
WAREHAM BOTTLE (Goss Record. 8th Edition: Page 21) *Matching Arms: WAREHAM*		67mm	3.50	7.50

for WARWICK – GUY'S PORRIDGE POT
see Guy's Porridge Pot

WATERLOOVILLE SOLDIER'S WATER BOTTLE (Goss Record. 8th Edition: Page 24) *Matching Arms: WATERLOOVILLE*		83mm	8.75	16.00

for WELSH CORACLE
see Llangollen Coracle

Any Welsh arms may be considered matching on Welsh models

Model			With any Arms	With Matching Arms
WELSH CROCHON (Goss Record. 8th Edition: Page 39) also see chapter headed 'POSTCARDS' *Matching Arms: CONWAY*		50mm 61mm 76mm 107mm	4.50 5.50 15.25 21.75	8.25 11.00 21.75 30.00
WELSH FISH BASKET *Matching Arms: ARMS OF WALES*		58mm		40.00
WELSH HAT *Matching Arms: ARMS OF WALES*	(a) Plain (b) Llanfair P.G. on brim	Dia.74mm	7.50 27.50	12.50 43.50
WELSH JACK AND LID (Goss Record. 8th Edition: Page 39) This model is not complete without its lid, value £8.00 *Matching Arms: ARMS OF WALES*		120mm	14.50	19.50
WELSH LEEK (Goss Record. 8th Edition: Page 39) *Matching Arms: ARMS OF WALES*		90mm	8.75	11.00
WELSH MILK CAN AND LID (Goss Record. 8th Edition: Page 39) This model is incomplete without its lid which is worth £7.00 *Matching Arms: ARMS OF WALES*		70mm 108mm 140mm	8.50 11.75 15.25	12.00 15.25 19.50

Model		With any Arms £ p	With Matching Arms £ p
WELSH PICYN (Goss Record. 8th Edition: Page 39) *Matching Arms: ARMS OF WALES*	62mm	7.00	11.00
for WELSH PORRIDGE BOWL see Welsh Picyn			
WENSLEYDALE LEYBURN LEATHER JACK (Goss record. 8th Edition: Page 38) *Matching Arms: LEYBURN*	67mm	4.50	12.50

WESTMINSTER ABBEY CORONATION CHAIR
(Goss Record. 8th Edition: Page 29)
see also CORONATION CHAIR (PERTH)

(a) White	87mm	26.00	37.50
(b) Stone in brown	87mm	82.50	110.00
(c) Brown	87mm	260.00	275.00
(d) Blue	87mm	Unpriced	

A blue version is thought to exist but has not yet
been sighted.
Matching Arms: WESTMINSTER ABBEY

WEYMOUTH ROMAN VASE (Goss Record. 8th Edition: Page 21) and advertisement page 61) *Matching Arms: WEYMOUTH*	56mm 94mm	4.00 8.75	7.50 11.00
for WHISKY CUP see National Highland Cuach or Whiksy Cup			
WHITBY AMMONITE (Goss Record. 7th Edition: Page 52 – Illustrated) Identical to the (rarer) Lyme Regis Ammonite *Matching Arms: WHITBY*	73mm	16.00	21.50
WHITBY PILLION STONE (Goss Record. 9th Edition: Page 33) *Matching Arms: WHITBY*	Length 72mm	16.00	19.50
for WHITLEY BAY, ST. MARY'S LIGHTHOUSE see St. Mary's Lighthouse, Whitley Bay			
WHITSTABLE ROMAN PATERA (Goss Record. 8th Edition: Page 27) *Matching Arms: WHITSTABLE*	Dia. 88mm	6.50	16.00

Wilderspool Roman Tetinae

Winchester Bushel

Winchester Flagon

Winchester Jack

Winchester Pot

Winchester Quart

Winchester Warden's Horn on Stand

Winchester Warden's Horn

Windsor Round Tower

Windsor Urn

Windsor Kettle and Lid

Windleshaw Chantry

Model		With any Arms £ p	With Matching Arms £ p
WILDERSPOOL ROMAN TETINAE	105mm		70.00
International League Model for 1924			
Correct Arms: THE INTERNATIONAL LEAGUE OF GOSS COLLECTORS .			
WINCHESTER BUSHEL	38mm	65.00	110.00
(Goss Record. 8th Edition: Page 24)	51mm	87.50	175.00
Matching Arms: WINCHESTER	58mm	200.00	475.00
WINCHESTER FLAGON	100mm	10.50	24.75
This model is not listed in any edition of the Goss	130mm	15.25	24.75

WINCHESTER FLAGON (continued)
This model is not listed in any edition of the Goss
Record. It is an un-named historical shape and
traditional to the Winchester Agent who stocked this
shape manufactured by the Copeland works until Goss
set up on his own and was able to meet his require-
ments.
See also PARIAN WARE C.
Matching Arms: WINCHESTER

for WINCHESTER BLACK JACK
see Winchester Jack

Model		With any Arms £ p	With Matching Arms £ p
WINCHESTER JACK	32mm	17.50	24.50
(Goss Record. 8th Edition: Page 23)	44mm	4.50	7.50
Matching Arms: WINCHESTER	83mm	8.75	16.00
	121mm	19.50	32.50
WINCHESTER POT	74mm	11.00	24.50
(Goss Record. 8th Edition: Page 24)			
Matching Arms: WINCHESTER			

WINCHESTER QUART — 92mm† — 350.00
(Goss Record. 8th Edition: Page 24)
This model is not known bearing a coat of arms. It is
a most impressive piece – rare and desirable.

WINCHESTER CASTLE WARDEN'S HORN	Length		
(Goss Record. 8th Edition: Page 24) (a) on plinth†	152mm	300.00	
Found named as Warder's or (b) without†	152mm	175.00	
Warden's Horn			

A beautiful piece in either form which
carries no arms.

Model			With any Arms £ p	With Matching Arms £ p
WINDLESHAW CHANTRY		128mm	65.00	130.00

On the base it is stated that this was a souvenir
of the 1920 Church Bazaar. (Near St. Helens, Lancs.)
Matching Arms: "En Dieu Et Mon Esperance"
(Sir Thomas Gerard of Kingsley & Bryn)

WINDSOR KETTLE (and lid)		170mm	95.00	117.50

(Goss Record. 8th Edition: Page 17)
Also known as Queen Charlotte's favourite
Windsor Kettle.
Matching Arms: WINDSOR

for WINDSOR – QUEEN CHARLOTTE'S
  FAVOURITE
see Windsor Kettle

WINDSOR ROUND TOWER (a) Large white[†]		145mm	425.00	
Two-piece, unglazed night-light (b) Large brown[†]		145mm	650.00	
(c) Large grey[†]		145mm	525.00	

(This model is illustrated in the
  Goss Record, 9th Edition: Page 40,
  Plate 1)

WINDSOR URN		38mm	3.50	6.50
(Goss Record. 8th Edition: Page 16)		82mm	7.00	11.00

Matching Arms: WINDSOR

WINSFORD SALT LUMP	(a)	80mm		43.50
This is identical to the Cheshire Salt Block, and	(b)	80mm		50.00

and appears with the Arms of Winsford either glazed or
unglazed. A rare variety (b) has been seen with holes
for pouring in the top and 'SALT' in script on the front.

WISBECH JUG		82mm	16.50	24.50

(Goss Record. 8th Edition: Page 17)
Matching Arms: WISBECH

WITCH'S CAULDRON		Length	10.50	11.00
(Goss Record. 9th Edition: Page 30)		47mm		

This model is identical to the Peterborough Tripod and
carries a quotation from Macbeth.
Matching with either Scottish or Shakespeare's arms.

WORCESTER JUG		64mm	4.50	8.25
(Goss Record. 8th Edition: Page 38)		101mm	8.75	12.50

Matching Arms: WORCESTER

Wisbech Jug

Winsford Salt Lump

Witch's Cauldron

Worcester Jug

Wymondham Jar

Yarmouth Ewer

Yarmouth Jug

York Roman Ewer

York Roman Urn

York Roman Vessel

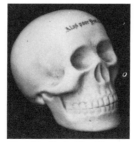

Yorick's Skull (Small)

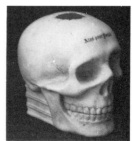

Yorick's Skull (Large)
Two-piece Nightlight

115

Model		With any Arms £ p	With Matching Arms £ p
WYMONDHAM ANCIENT JAR (Goss Record. 8th Edition: Page 29) *Matching Arms: WYMONDHAM*	61mm	6.50	12.50
YARMOUTH EWER (Goss Record. 8th Edition: Page 29) *Matching Arms: GREAT YARMOUTH*	62mm	3.50	7.00
YARMOUTH JUG (Goss Record. 8th Edition: Page 29 and advertisement page 77) *Matching Arms: GREAT YARMOUTH*	132mm	35.00	56.50

YORICK'S SKULL
(Goss Record. 8th Edition: Page 35)

(a) Pale yellow†	38mm	30.00	
(b) White unglazed †	70mm	82.50	
(c) Pale yellow†	70mm	95.00	
(d) White unglazed†	102mm	110.00	
(e) Pale yellow†	102mm	175.00	
(f) White glazed†	102mm	130.00	

Note: the 102mm version is in two pieces and can be used as a night-light.

Model		With any Arms £ p	With Matching Arms £ p
YORK ROMAN EWER (Goss Record. 8th Edition: Page 38) see also Chapter headed 'POSTCARDS' *Matching Arms: YORK*	63mm 127mm	3.50 11.00	7.50 19.50
YORK ROMAN URN (Goss Record. 8th Edition: Page 38) *Matching Arms: YORK*	51mm 101mm	3.25 10.50	6.50 14.50
YORK ROMAN VESSEL (Goss Record. 8th Edition: Page 38) *Matching Arms: YORK*	73mm	8.50	12.00

Cottages, Houses, Churches etc.

Cottages are amongst the most desirable and sought after products of the Goss factory. The first seven cottages were nightlights, being introduced in 1893 by Adolphus Goss.

Smaller versions of these were subsequently produced and the range of cottages was extended so that when manufacture ceased in the early 1930's, no less than forty had been marketed, excluding variations and differing sizes. Several new models were in preparation at the end, and Plas Newydd, Atlantic View Hotel and Massachusetts Hall have never been seen, except for a white glazed and 'Blackpool' crested second in the case of the last-named. Could this have been a prototype that never went into production?

Cottages are listed here alphabetically by person, associated town, or title. Buildings which are not listed here will be found in the Named Models or Goss England Chapters.

Most earlier cottages appear either glazed or unglazed but post 1914 examples are generally unglazed only. Some collectors prefer glazed models and £5.00–£10.00 should be added to the prices given for such varieties.

Not surprisingly, many variations in the models occurred during the years that they were in production. For example, if a building was altered then the alterations would be faithfully reproduced when the next batch of models was ordered from the factory. Charles Dickens' House, Gads Hill is a good example of this, for when the ivy was cut away from either side of the front porch, a pair of small windows was discovered and these were then incorporated into the model.

Other variations include the Goss Oven appearing with either an orange or a brown roof, the First and Last House with either a cream or grey roof and the Look-Out House, Newquay with four or five circular windows.

Minor variations in colour may be disregarded as over the years many different batches of paint were used.

Bunyan's Cottage, Elstow

Burns' Cottage, small

Burns' Cottage, nightlight

Buxton, Cat and Fiddle Inn

*Old Court House,
Christchurch*

*Dickens' House, Rochester,
without Porch Windows*

*First and Last House with
Annexe*

*First and Last House, Land's
End*

*Dickens' House, Rochester,
with Porch Windows*

*First and Last Post Office,
Sennen*

*Glastonbury, Church of Joseph
of Arimathoea*

Goss Oven, Stoke-on-Trent

118

£   p

for ABBOT'S KITCHEN, GLASTONBURY ABBEY
see Glastonbury Abbey, Abbot's Kitchen

for ANN HATHAWAY'S COTTAGE, SHOTTERY
see Hathaway's Cottage, Shottery

for ATLANTIC VIEW HOTEL, LAND'S END
see Land's End, Atlantic View Hotel

for BEDDGELERT, PRINCE LLEWELLYN'S HOUSE
see Prince Llewellyn's House, Beddgelert

for BOURNEMOUTH, PORTMAN LODGE
see Portman Lodge, Bournemouth

(JOHN) BUNYAN'S COTTAGE, ELSTOW   Length   60mm   740.00

(ROBERT) BURNS' COTTAGE, AYR
(Goss Record. 8th Edition: Page 40)
Found either glazed or unglazed
      (a) Small   62mm   60.00
      (b) Night-light (white windows with brown glazing bars) 145mm   120.00
      (c) as (b) but with no windows   145mm   130.00

BUXTON, CAT AND FIDDLE INN   Length   65mm   195.00

for CHARLES DICKENS' HOUSE, GADS HILL PLACE
see (Charles) Dickens' House, Gads Hill

CHRISTCHURCH, OLD COURT HOUSE   Length   76mm   250.00
(Not listed in any version of the Goss Records, but advertised by
Ritchie & Co. on the back cover of the Eighth Edition.)

for COCKERMOUTH, WORDSWORTH'S HOUSE
see Wordsworth's Birthplace, Cockermouth

for COURTHOUSE, CHRISTCHURCH
see Christchurch Old Court House

**(CHARLES) DICKENS' HOUSE, GADS HILL,
ROCHESTER**   65mm   100.00
(Goss Record. 8th Edition: Page 27)
There are two varieties of this model – with and without
small windows on either side of the front door. The value is
unaffected.

for 'DOVE COTTAGE', GRASMERE
see (William) Wordsworth's Home, 'Dove Cottage', Grasmere

£ p

for ELLEN TERRY'S FARM, TENTERDEN, KENT
see (Miss Ellen) Terry's Farm, Tenterden, Kent

FIRST AND LAST HOUSE IN ENGLAND
(Goss Record. 8th Edition: Page 18)
Can be found with a badge on one end, add £10.00 for this.
The small model can be found with either a green or black door.
Also found glazed.

(a) Small, cream roof, green door	64mm	60.00
(b) Small, grey roof, black door	64mm	65.00
(c) Night-light, cream roof, green door	117mm	195.00
(d) Night-light, grey roof, black door	117mm	195.00
(e) Night-light, white roof, green door	117mm	215.00

FIRST AND LAST HOUSE IN ENGLAND – WITH ANNEXE
Length 150mm 525.00

FIRST AND LAST POST OFFICE IN ENGLAND SENNEN
(Goss Record. 8th Edition: Page 18) Length 73mm 125.00
Sometimes has a badge on one end
for which £10.00 should be added.

GLASTONBURY ABBEY – THE ABBOT'S KITCHEN 88mm 525.00
(Goss Record. 9th Edition: Pages 26 & 27)
Can be found with either black or red door.

GLASTONBURY – CHURCH OF JOSEPH OF ARIMATHOEA
70mm 565.00

GOSS OVEN Length 75mm
(Goss Record. 9th Edition: Pages 27 & 28. Plate G)
There are two varieties: (a) Orange Roof 160.00
The ovens were situated in Sturgess Street, (b) Brown Roof 175.00
Stoke-on-Trent and are still standing today.

for GRETNA GREEN, OLD TOLL BAR
see Old Toll Bar, Gretna Green

GULLANE SMITHY Length 75mm 475.00
(Goss Record. 9th Edition: Page 14)

(THOMAS) HARDY'S BIRTHPLACE Length 100mm 305.00
(Goss Record. 9th Edition: Page 14)

Glastonbury Abbey, Abbot's Kitchen

Gullane Smithy

Thomas Hardy's Birthplace

Ann Hathaway's Cottage, small

Ann Hathaway's Cottage, large

Holden Chapel, Boston, U.S.A.

Hop Kiln, Headcorn

Dr. Johnson's House, Lichfield

The Feathers Hotel, Ledbury

Old Market House, Ledbury

Lloyd George's Early Home without Annexe

Lloyd George's Early Home with Annexe

121

£ p

(ANN) HATHAWAY'S COTTAGE, SHOTTERY

(Goss Record. 8th Edition: Page 35) (a) Small   62mm   52.50
Also found glazed.   (b) Night-light   148mm   130.00
               (c) Night-light, white,
                   unglazed   148mm   195.00

This model was in constant production from
the mid-1890s and minor variations will be
found as moulds were replaced. These
variations do not affect values. For later
examples see GOS ENGLAND

for HEADCORN HOP KILN
see Hop Kiln, Headcorn, Kent

HOLDEN CHAPEL, HARVARD UNIVERSITY, BOSTON, USA.
(Goss Record. 8th Edition: Page 43)   Length 137mm   1300.00

HOP KILN, HEADCORN, KENT
(Goss Record. 9th Edition: Page 20)   Height 89mm   1100.00

for HUER'S HOUSE
see Newquay Huer's House

for ISAAC WALTON'S COTTAGE or BIRTHPLACE, SHALLOWFORD
see Walton's Cottage, (Birthplace), Shallowford

for JOHN BUNYAN'S COTTAGE, ELSTOW
see Bunyan's Cottage, Elstow

(DR. SAMUEL) JOHNSON'S HOUSE, LICHFIELD   75mm   115.00
(Goss Record. 8th Edition: Page 32)
Also found glazed.

for JOHN KNOX'S HOUSE
see GOSS ENGLAND chapter

LAND'S END, ATLANTIC VIEW HOTEL   Unpriced
(Goss Record. 8th Edition: Page 18)
Although this model was listed as being 'in the course of
preparation' in the Eighth Edition, it was apparently never
produced, and was omitted from the Ninth Edition.

LEDBURY – THE FEATHERS HOTEL   Length
Rumour has it that the Hotel owner purchased   114mm   650.00
the entire output of this model, and presented
them to couples 'honeymooning' at the Hotel.

LEDBURY – OLD MARKET HOUSE   Length 68mm   240.00
(Goss Record. 9th Edition: Page 18. Plate H)

£ p

for LLANGOLLEN, PLAS NEWYDD
see Plas Newydd, Llangollen

for LLEWELLYN'S HOUSE, BEDDGELERT
see Prince Llewellyn's House, Beddgelert

(RT. HON.) LLOYD GEORGE'S EARLY HOME Length 62mm 115.00
(Goss Record. 8th Edition: Page 39)

(RT. HON.) LLOYD GEORGE'S EARLY HOME Length 101mm 95.00
– WITH ANNEXE

for LOOK-OUT HOUSE
see Newquay Look-Out House

MANX COTTAGE	(a) Small	Length 62mm	75.00
(Goss Record. 8th Edition: Page 26)	(b) Night-light	Length 122mm	125.00

MASSACHUSETTS HALL, HARVARD UNIVERSITY,
BOSTON, U.S.A. Length 170mm 1500.00
(Goss Record. 8th Edition: Page 43)
The only variety known to exist is white
glazed and bears the Blackpool arms –
there must have been coloured examples
made – keep looking!

NEWQUAY – HUER'S HOUSE			
(Goss Record. 8th Edition: Page 18)	(a) Grey	Length 70mm	82.50
Also found glazed	(b) White		46.50

NEWQUAY – LOOK-OUT HOUSE	(a) 4 windows	65mm	75.00
(Goss Record. 8th Edition: Page 18)	(b) 5 windows	65mm	75.00

for OLD COURTHOUSE, CHRISTCHURCH
see Christchurch, Old Courthouse

OLD MAIDS' COTTAGE, LEE
(Goss Record. 8th Edition: Page 20) Length 73mm 105.00
Also found glazed

for OLD MARKET HOUSE, LEDBURY
see Ledbury – Old Market House

for OLD SMITHY, GULLANE
see Gullane Smithy

OLD THATCHED COTTAGE, POOLE Length 68mm 305.00
(Goss Record. 9th Edition: Page 14)

Manx Cottage

Huer's House, Newquay

Look-out House, Newquay

Old Maids' Cottage, Lee, Devon

Old Thatched Cottage, Poole

Old Toll Bar, Gretna Green

Portman Lodge, Bournemouth

Priest's House, Prestbury

Prince Llewellyn's House, Beddgelert

St. Catherine's Chapel, Abbotsbury

St. Nicholas Chapel, Lantern Hill, Ilfracombe

St. Nicholas Chapel, St. Ives

£ p

OLD TOLL BAR, GRETNA GREEN   Length 125mm   1300.00

PLAS NEWYDD, LLANGOLLEN   Unpriced
(Goss Record. 8th Edition: Page 39)
It is said that seven of these models were
produced, and sold by the local agent.
Apparently no more were made, and none
have as yet been discovered.

for POOLE, OLD THATCHED COTTAGE
see Old Thatched Cottage, Poole

PORTMAN LODGE, BOURNEMOUTH   84mm × 72mm   305.00
Appears with either open or closed door

for PRESTBURY, PRIEST'S HOUSE
see Priest's House, Prestbury

PRIEST'S HOUSE, PRESTBURY   Height 71mm   875.00
This model is marked 'copyright' and
numbered 786

PRINCE LLEWELLYN'S HOUSE, BEDDGELERT   63mm   95.00
(Goss Record. 8th Edition: Page 38)
Also found glazed

ST. CATHERINE'S CHAPEL, ABBOTSBURY   Length 87mm   350.00
(Goss Record. 9th Edition: Page 14)

for ST. IVES, ANCIENT CHAPEL OF ST. NICHOLAS
see St. Nicholas Chapel, St. Ives

ST. NICHOLAS CHAPEL, LANTERN HILL, ILFRACOMBE
(Goss Record. 8th Edition: Page 20)   74mm   115.00
Also found glazed

ST. NICHOLAS CHAPEL, ST. IVES
          (a) White, glazed   55mm   95.00
          (b) Coloured, glazed or unglazed   175.00

Shakespeare's House, small

Shakespeare's House, Half-length

Shakespeare's House, Two-piece Nightlight

Southampton Tudor House

Sulgrave Manor

Ellen Terry's Farm, Tenterden, Kent

Isaac Walton's Birthplace, Shallowford

A Window in Thrums small

A Window in Thrums Nightlight

Wordsworth's Birthplace, Cockermouth

Wordsworth's Home, Dove Cottage, Grasmere

Massachusett's Hall, Harvard University

£ p

SHAKESPEARE'S HOUSE
(Goss Record. 8th Edition: Page 35)
Many variations in size may be found.
These are the only models made from
GOSS moulds: for all other sizes
see GOSS ENGLAND models.

		Length	
(a) Small. Full-length		68mm	50.00
(b) Small. Full-length		78mm	52.50
(c) Medium. Full-length		110mm	60.00
(d) Medium. Full-length		140mm	70.00
(e) Night-light. Full-length		180mm	135.00
(f) Small. Half-length		82mm	70.00
(g) Large. Half-length		95mm	85.00
(h) Large. Half-length. Separate base		109mm	90.00

SOUTHAMPTON TUDOR HOUSE   Length 83mm   245.00
(Goss Record. 8th Edition: Page 23)

SULGRAVE MANOR   Overall length 125mm   875.00
(Goss Record. 8th Edition: Page 30)

(MISS ELLEN) TERRY'S FARM, TENTERDEN, KENT
(Goss Record. 8th Edition: Page 27)   Length 70mm   285.00

for THOMAS HARDY'S HOUSE
see Hardy's Birthplace

(ISAAC) WALTON'S COTTAGE (BIRTHPLACE), SHALLOWFORD
There are two sizes of this model,   (a) 86mm   455.00
but the variations are minimal   (b) 95mm   675.00

"WINDOW IN THRUMS"   (a) Small   60mm   95.00
(Goss Record. 8th Edition: Page 40)   (b) Night-light   130mm   195.00
Both varieties also found glazed
This cottage in Kirriemuir was the
subject of a novel by author J.M. Barrie

(WILLIAM) WORDSWORTH'S BIRTHPLACE, COCKERMOUTH
(Goss Record. 8th Edition: Page 18)   81mm   195.00

(WILLIAM) WORDSWORTH'S HOME, 'DOVE COTTAGE',
GRASMERE   Length 102mm   350.00
(Goss Record. 9th Edition: Page 31)

Crosses

No Crosses, except Richmond Market Place Cross, bear any arms at all.

Model				With any Arms £ p	With Matching Arms £ p
BANBURY CROSS See GOSS ENGLAND					
BAKEWELL ANCIENT CROSS	(a) White	145mm		170.00	
(Goss Record. 8th Edition: Page 18)	(b) Brown	145mm		220.00	
BUXTON, OLD MARKET CROSS	Grey	88mm		1300.00	
CAMPBELTOWN ANCIENT CROSS	Brown	152mm		485.00	
(Goss Record. 8th Edition: Page 40)					
CAREW ANCIENT CROSS					
(Goss Record. 9th Edition: Page 34)					
	(a) White unglazed	150mm		87.50	
	(b) Brown	150mm		87.50	
	(c) White glazed	216mm		130.00	
	(d) Brown	216mm		220.00	
EYAM ANCIENT CROSS					
(Goss Record. 8th Edition: Page 18)					
	(a) White glazed	168mm		130.00	
	(b) White unglazed	168mm		175.00	
	(c) Brown	168mm		265.00	
INVERARY – ANCIENT CROSS OF THE NOBLES					
(Goss Record. 8th Edition: Page 40)	Brown	141mm		525.00	
for IONA CROSS					
see St. Martin's Cross, Iona					
KIRK BRADDAN CROSS					
(Goss Record. 8th Edition: Page 26)					
	(a) Brown	84mm		65.00	
	(b) White unglazed	84mm		175.00	

Bakewell Cross

Buxton Market Cross

Campbeltown Cross

Carew Cross

Eyam Cross

Inverary Cross of the Nobles

St. Martins Cross, Iona

Kirk Braddan Cross

Llandaff Cross

Richmond Market Place Cross

St. Buryan Cross

St. Columb Major Cross

129

Model			With any Arms £ p	With Matching Arms £ p
LLANDAFF ANCIENT CROSS				
(Goss Record. 8th Edition: Page 39)				
(a) White unglazed		147mm	240.00	
(b) Brown		147mm	400.00	
RICHMOND MARKET PLACE CROSS				
(Goss Record. 8th Edition: Page 38)				
(a) White glazed		130mm	30.00	40.00
(b) Brown		130mm	265.00	
Matching Arms: RICHMOND (YORKS)				
ST. BURYAN ANCIENT CROSS				
(a) White glazed		43mm	52.50	
(b) White unglazed		43mm	65.00	
(c) Brown		43mm	87.50	
ST. COLUMB MAJOR ANCIENT CROSS				
(Goss Record. 8th Edition: Page 18)				
(a) White glazed		90mm	43.50	
(b) White unglazed		90mm	56.50	
(c) Brown		90mm	110.00	
Variety (a) can be found with the Blackpool arms which will halve its value.				
ST. IVES ANCIENT CROSS	(a) White	140mm	175.00	
(Goss Record. 8th Edition: Page 18)	(b) Brown	140mm	265.00	
	(c) White	204mm	200.00	
	(d) Brown	204mm	265.00	
ST. MARTIN'S CROSS, IONA				
(Goss Record. 8th Edition: Page 40)				
(a) White glazed, flat back		142mm	82.50	
(b) Brown		142mm	130.00	
(c) White glazed, flat back		216mm	130.00	
(d) Brown		216mm	175.00	
SANDBACH CROSSES				
(Goss Record. 8th Edition: Page 17)		260mm	1100.00	
This model is made in three sections, the two brown crosses being held in place by cork plugs.				

Fonts

Model			With any Arms £ p	With Matching Arms £ p

AVEBURY ANCIENT SAXON FONT (CALNE)
(Goss Record. 8th Edition: Page 91 –
  photo and advertisement) (a) White glazed | 86mm | 87.50 | 130.00
Matching Arms: CALNE (b) Brown † | 86mm | 300.00 |

BUCKLAND MONACHORUM FONT 75mm | | 350.00
Matching Arms: BUCKLAND ABBEY, Nr YELVERTON

for CALNE FONT
see Avebury Ancient Saxon Font

for CANTERBURY FONT
see St. Martin's Church Font, Canterbury

HADDON HALL NORMAN FONT
(Goss Record. 8th Edition: Page 18)
  (a) White glazed | 92mm | 43.50 | 56.90
  (b) Brown † | 92mm | 265.00 |
Matching Arms: MATLOCK BATH or BAKEWELL

HEREFORD CATHEDRAL FONT
(Goss Record. 8th Edition: (a) White glazed | 96mm | 105.00 | 110.00
  Page 66 and advertisement) (b) Brown | 96mm | 265.00 | 265.00
*Matching Arms: HEREFORD CATHEDRAL or SEE
OF HEREFORD A.D. 1275*

**for LLANTWIT MAJOR NORMAN FONT IN ST.
  ILTYD'S CHURCH**
see St. Iltyd's Church Font (Llantwit Major)

for MONMOUTH FONT
see Warwick Font, Troy House, Monmouth

ST. ILTYD'S CHURCH FONT (LLANTWIT MAJOR)
(Goss Record. 8th Edition: Page 39)
  (a) Brown † | 88mm | 435.00
  (b) White unglazed † | 88mm | 875.00
  (c) White glazed, Blackpool Arms | 88mm | 300.00

Avebury Ancient Saxon Font (Calne)

Buckland Monachorum Font

Haddon Hall Norman Font

Hereford Cathedral Font

St. Iltyd's Church Font, Llantwit Major

St. Ives Church Font

St. Martins Font, Canterbury, Closed

St. Martins Font, Canterbury, Dished

St. Martins Font, Canterbury, Open

St. Tudno's Church Font

Southwell Catherdral Font

Stratford-on-Avon Church Font

Model			With any Arms £ p	With Matching Arms £ p
ST. IVES CHURCH ANCIENT FONT				
(Goss Record. 8th Edition: Page 18)				
	(a) White glazed	88mm	21.50	43.50
	(b) White unglazed †	88mm	87.50	
	(c) Brown †	88mm	130.00	
Matching Arms: ST. IVES (CORNWALL)				
ST. MARTIN'S CHURCH FONT, CANTERBURY				
(Goss Record. 8th Edition: Page 26)				
	(a) lidded, white glazed †	75mm	38.00	
	(b) lidded, white unglazed †	75mm	65.00	
	(c) lidded, brown †	75mm	87.50	
	(d) dished, white glazed	69mm	35.00	40.00
	(e) open, white glazed †	74mm	35.00	
	(f) open, brown †	74mm	87.50	
There are three varieties of this font: Lidded, dished, and open.				
Matching Arms: City or See of CANTERBURY				
ST. TUDNO'S CHURCH FONT, LLANDUDNO				
(Goss Record. 8th Edition: Photo & advertisement)				
	(a) White glazed	95mm	21.75	26.00
	(b) White unglazed	95mm	43.50	
	(c) Brown †	95mm	175.00	
Matching Arms: LLANDUDNO				
for SHAKESPEARE'S FONT				
see Stratford-on-Avon Church Font				
SOUTHWELL CATHEDRAL FONT				
(Goss Record. 8th Edition: Page 30)				
	(a) White glazed	95mm	65.00	
	(b) White unglazed	95mm	87.50	
	(c) Brown †	95mm	220.00	
STRATFORD-ON-AVON CHURCH FONT				
(Goss Record. 8th Edition: Page 35)				
	(a) White unglazed	54mm	17.50	24.50
	(b) Brown †	54mm	300.00	

The following inscription appears inside bowl in Gothic lettering surrounding arms:
Model of font in which Shakespeare was baptized
Matching Arms: STRATFORD-ON-AVON CHURCH
or SHAKESPEARE'S ARMS

Model	With any Arms £ p	With Matching Arms £ p

for TROY HOUSE FONT
see Warwick Font, Troy House, Monmouth

WARWICK FONT, TROY HOUSE, MONMOUTH
(Goss Record. 8th Edition: Page 36)

(a) White glazed †	55mm	43.50
(b) White unglazed †	55mm	43.50
(c) White glazed but with coloured shields †	55mm	43.50
(d) Brown †	55mm	175.00

WINCHESTER CATHEDRAL FONT

(a) White glazed †	400.00
(b) White unglazed †	485.00
(c) Black †	650.00

This model was made in two sizes: Heights 115mm
and 134mm. Same value.

Animals

This series of animals was produced later than most other pieces, mostly during the early 20s. Many models were first introduced for sale at the British Empire Exhibition at Wembley in 1924/25 and the majority of animals will be found with either the 1924 or 1925 exhibition arms. Early animals will be found in the PARIAN chapter.

Model			With any Arms £ p	With Matching Arms £ p
AYLESBURY DUCK *Matching Arms: AYLESBURY*		Length 100mm	175.00	195.00
BEAR, Polar	(a) Glazed (b) Unglazed		285.00 175.00	
for BEAR AND RAGGED STAFF see PARIAN (B) chapter				
BULL *Any Spanish arms could be considered matching*		Length 135mm	300.00	400.00
CALF *Possible matching arms: COWES*		Length 117mm	265.00	300.00
CHESHIRE CAT (Goss Record. 9th Edition: Page 11, Plate M)	(a) Glazed (b) Unglazed	Length 83mm	65.00 87.50	110.00
Inscribed 'He grins like a Cheshire Cat chewing gravel'. This cat often has a firing flaw in one or both ears, which reduces the price by around one-third. *Matching Arms: CHESHIRE*				
COW *Possible Matching Arms: COWES*		Length 135mm	300.00	350.00
DOG See also Prince Llewellyn's Dog		Length 133mm	300.00	
HIPPOPOTAMUS	Length	127mm	300.00	
KANGAROO		94mm	485.00	

Sandbach Crosses　　　*St. Ives Cross*　　　*Warwick Font, Troy House, Monmouth*

Winchester Cathedral Font　　　*Aylesbury Duck*　　　*Polar Bear*

Bull　　　*Calf*　　　*Cheshire Cat*

Cow　　　*Dog*　　　*Hippopotamus*

Model			With any Arms £ p	With Matching Arms £ p
LION (Standing)	Length	135mm	265.00	

LION, LUCERNE
(Goss Record. 9th Edition: Page 38)

(a) White glazed & crested (at front or rear, usually Blackpool)	Length 110mm		26.00	70.00
(b) White glazed with Latin wording	110mm		65.00†	
(c) White unglazed with wording	110mm		87.50	130.00
(d) Brown	110mm		265.00†	

This model should have a spear protruding $\frac{1}{4}''$ out of
the centre of the back. Often the spear is broken off
level with the lion's back in manufacture and is glazed
over. Beasts without the $\frac{1}{4}''$ spear are worth some 50%
less than the varieties priced here.
Matching Arms: LUCERNE

for LION (WEMBLEY)
see Wembley Lion

for LUCERNE LION
see Lion, Lucerne

PENGUIN	Length			
Matching Arms: FALKLAND ISLANDS	83mm		265.00	300.00

The strong Goss family connection with the Falkland
Islands probably prompted the appearance of this
model.

PRINCE LLEWELLYN'S DOG – GELERT	Length			
This is an identical model to the DOG listed above, but coloured, and named on the plinth.	133mm		435.00	

RACEHORSE	Length			
Possible Matching Arms: NEWMARKET	120mm		300.00	375.00

RHINOCEROS	Length 129mm		300.00	

SHEEP	(a) Early	Length 105mm	See PARIAN C	
	(b) On Plinth	Length 147mm	175.00	200.00

Possible correct arms would be those of any sheep
    farming areas, e.g. Tavistock

Kangaroo

Standing Lion

Lucerne Lion

Penguin

Prince Llewellyn's Dog, 'Gelert'

Racehorse

Rhinoceros

Sheep

Shetland Pony

Swan

Tiger

Wembley Lion

Model			With any Arms £ p	With Matching Arms £ p
SHETLAND PONY		Length		
(Goss Record. 9th Edition: Page 36)		103mm	130.00	175.00

The model also appears with arms of places on
Dartmoor and Exmoor and was obviously sold in
these areas as a model of a local pony.
Matching Arms: LERWICK

SWAN

(a)		60mm	70.00	
(b)		73mm	75.00	
(c)		94mm	87.50	
(d) Glazed. approx.		120mm	110.00	
(e) Unglazed. approx.		120mm	110.00	

Can be either a cream jug or posy vase. Occasionally
found with arms or decorations to rear. Same value.

TIGER on rocky base (a) White	Length 170mm	550.00	
(b) Coloured[+]	Length 170mm	850.00	

WEMBLEY LION (made for the B.E.E. 1925)

Matching Arms: B.E.E. 1925	Length 100mm	110.00	157.00

Domestic and Ornamental Ware

This, the most difficult chapter of the guide, has been revised to allow greater clarity, and a substantial number of additional photographs have been included so that very few pieces are not now illustrated.

These improvements should assist the reader in finding difficult to place items, but please look under Parian Ware (C) and Goss England if an item cannot be found here.

Whenever possible given names for types of wares have been taken from the *Goss Records*, the compiler of which, J. J. Jarvis, obtained information from the Goss factory in later years, so that in the absence of any official catalogues, these records provide the only listings of pieces on sale at the time.

The most notable items to have come to light recently are two 61-piece dinner services which were made for the Goss agent in Malta. Upon his death they passed to his two daughters living in England. Made from pottery and not originating from the Goss factory, each piece carries the arms of Malta and comprises:

One soup tureen and cover with base plate
Two vegetable dishes and covers with base plates
One gravy boat and stand
One cheese dish and cover
Twelve dinner plates
Twelve side plates
Twelve soup dishes
Twelve dessert bowls

Approximate value   £300.00

A. Table Ware

BAGWARE TEA SERVICE: £ p

This ware is in the form of a tied bag, gathered in by a blue cord
with gilded tassels and having a matching blue cord handle.

Cup and Saucer	50mm	11.00
	60mm	11.00
Cream Jug	60mm	10.00
	75mm	10.00
Milk Jug	114mm	17.50
Slop Bowl	Dia. 110mm	11.00
	Dia. 140mm	14.50
Sugar Basin	55mm	11.00
Jam Dish and Lid	86mm	16.00
Marmalade Dish and Lid	86mm	16.00
Preserve Jar and Lid	100mm	11.00
Tea Pot	115mm	30.00
	140mm	30.00
	155mm	35.00
Cord not blue 60mm		15.25
Tea Plate	100mm	5.25
	125mm	5.25
	135mm	5.25
	150mm	5.25
Cake Plate	250mm	16.00

Add around £5.00 for each additional crest

TAPER TEA SERVICE:

Cup and Saucer	69mm	4.75
	82mm	4.75
	Miniature 38mm	6.50
Cream Jug	81mm	4.75
	85mm	4.75
	95mm	5.25

Late Cup and Saucer

Late Cup and Saucer

High Melon Cup and Saucer

Late Cup and Saucer

Bagware Cup and Saucer

Low Melon Cup and Saucer

Late Tea Plate

Bagware Tea Plate

Melon Tea Plate

Late Tea Plate Side View

Bagware Tea Plate Side View

Melon Tea Plate Side View

142

		£ p
Milk Jug	108mm	5.50
	145mm	6.50
	159mm	8.75
	176mm	15.00
Slop Bowl	55mm	4.75
Sugar Basin	40mm	4.00
Tea Pot	112mm	19.50
	140mm	26.00
Coffee Pot often named Taper Coffee Pot	160mm	20.00

MELON-SHAPED TEA SERVICE:

Low Melon Cup and Saucer	44mm	4.75
	53mm	5.50
Melon Cup and Saucer	55mm	4.75
	75mm	5.50
High Melon Cup and Saucer	70mm	5.50
	115mm	6.50
Cream Jug	53mm	4.50
	60mm	4.75
	72mm	5.50
Milk Jug	85mm	5.50
	100mm	5.50
	118mm	7.00
Slop Bowl	48mm	4.75
Sugar Basin	42mm	3.50
	54mm	4.75
Tea Pot	93mm	19.50
	114mm	21.75
	140mm	26.00
Tea Plate	100mm	4.00
	130mm	4.00
	150mm	4.00
	160mm	4.00
Cake Plate	250mm	13.00

Add around £5.00 for each additional crest

Octagonal Coffee Cup and Saucer

Octagonal Sugar Bowl, Probably Late

Octagonal Coffee Pot and Lid

Porcelain Spoon

Octagonal Milk Jug

Manx Legs Teapot

Candlestick, Column 69mm

Hat Pin Holder

Melon Teapot and Lid

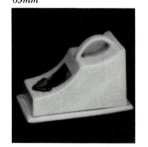

Rectangular Cheese Dish and Cover, Miniature

Slipper Wall Pocket

Taper Tea Pot and Lid

£ p

OCTAGONAL COFFEE SERVICE
With heavily gilded rims

Cup and Saucer	62mm	21.50
Milk Jug	77mm	21.50
Sugar Bowl	46mm	21.50
Coffee Pot	192mm	32.50

SUNDRY CUPS AND SAUCERS:

Coffee Can and Saucer	52mm	4.75
Straight-sided Cup and Saucer	70mm	4.50
Curved Cup and Saucer. Not early or late	70mm	4.50
Early Two-handled Straight-sided Cup and Saucer with two blue square handles	68mm	19.50

There are various other shapes of cup and saucer. Most of these
are late and tend to be somewhat heavy and wide. Styles
include those with curved rims or bases and many varieties of
straight-sided, fluted or decorated cups. The value of all
these is around £4.00 – £5.00

CREAM JUGS:

Ball-shaped	47mm	3.50
	55mm	4.50
	60mm	4.75
	65mm	7.50
Frilled	57mm	4.50
Ribbed	86mm	7.50
Kneeling – Manx legs and handle in yellow	67mm	17.50
Big-lipped	60mm	4.75
	67mm	5.50
Tankard with everted rim	67mm	4.75
Fluted	55mm	4.75
Urn-shaped with butterfly handle	65mm	11.00
Welsh Lady (Coloured)	94mm	26.00

Tankard Mug with Everted Rim Early

Tankard Cream Jug Early, Angular Handle

Ribbed Milk Jug

Tankard Mug with Everted Rim

Welsh Lady Cream Jug

Fluted Cream Jug

Tankard Mug, Early

Manx Legs Cream Jug

Big-lipped Cream Jug

Tankard Mug, Angular Handle

Urn-Shaped Cream Jug, Early, Butterfly Handle

Ball Cream Jug

Giant 176mm Taper Jug

Taper Coffee Pot

Taper Cup and Saucer

Taper Milk Jug

Bagware Teapot

Early Straight Sided Cup and Saucer

Shaped High Melon Milk Jug

Bagware Milk Jug

Coffee Can and Saucer

Shaped Low Melon Cream Jug

Bagware Cream Jug

Individual Morning Set

Ribbed Sugar Basin

Taper Sugar Basin

Early Teapot with Three Small Feet

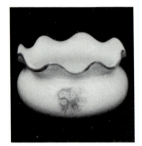

Fluted Sugar Basin

Melon Sugar Basin

Mug One Handle

Ball Shaped Sugar Basin

Bagware Sugar Basin

Beaker, Barrel-shaped, Early 74mm

Frilled Sugar Basin

Bagware Marmalade Dish and Lid

Barrel Shaped Mug

£ p

SUGAR BOWLS:

Ball-shaped	48mm	3.50
	55mm	4.50
Frilled	Dia. 50mm	4.50
Ribbed	58mm	5.50
	50mm	5.50
Kneeling – Manx legs in yellow	67mm	17.50
Crinkle	25mm	4.00
Fluted	40mm	4.75
Tapered	42mm	3.00
	48mm	4.00

TEA POTS:

Manx Legs	110mm	52.50
Add £20 for Manx arms		
Globular, having straight spout, curved handle, and 3 small feet	116mm	35.00

OTHER ITEMS OF TABLE WARE:

Beaker, cylindrical with everted rim	135mm	6.50
Butter dish with ears of corn in relief	Dia. 143mm	13.00
Butter Dish – "Waste not" and ears of corn in relief	Dia. 143mm	13.00
Butter Dish. With carved wooden surround	Dia. 150mm	8.50
Butter Dish and Cheese Dish – These are a pair with rounded lids, having dolphin handles Height 90mm	Dia. 152mm	13.00
Child's Feeding Bowl	Dia. 130mm	8.75
Egg Cup, Cylindrical	60mm	4.50
Egg Cup, Goblet	50mm	4.50
Several patterns, one scalloped	60mm	4.50
Egg Cup, Mounted on plate	62mm	6.50
Egg-shaped Mustard Pot	60mm	5.50

Butter Dish 'Waste Not'

Butter Dish, Ears of Corn in Relief

Tumbler

Cheese Dish and Cover with Dolphin Handle

Butter Dish and Cover with Dolphin Handle

Serviette Ring

Egg Cup, Goblet

Egg Cup on Plate 62mm

Egg Cup, Cylindrical

Salt Castor

Sugar Castor

Egg-shaped Cruet in Stand

		£ p
Egg-shaped Pepper Castor	60mm	5.00
Egg-shaped Salt Castor	60mm	5.00
The above three items are found also in a stand with tall handle Price Complete:	110mm	22.50
Fruit Basket. With coral handle	212mm	100.00
(Illustrated. Goss Record. 8th Edition: Page 4. Upper Shelf.) See also Parian C.		
Honey Section Dish – Square, with bee as knob on lid	140mm square	20.00
Individual Morning Set – Cup on elongated platter	203mm	20.00
Invalid Feeding Cup	76mm	10.00
Jam Dish	Dia. 145mm	5.25
Nut Tray	Dia. 125mm	4.50
Both above twelve-sided, fluted and frilled		
Milk Jug – Cylindrical	100mm	8.50
Plate, scallop edge	112mm	15.00
Preserve Jar and Lid – various fruits Dia. 57mm Height 100mm		10.00
Dia. 72mm Height 110mm		11.00

A number of these Jars were made with appropriately
decorated base-plates for which £10–£20 should be added.
NB The additional value added by the fruit decoration is
substantial. See *Goss China Arms and Decorations and Their
Values*, p. 100.

Preserve Pot and Lid in the shape of a timbered cottage with thatched roof	115mm	56.50
Tea Pot Stand. Round.	Dia. 82mm	4.00
	Dia. 102mm	5.25
	Dia. 118mm	5.50
	Dia. 144mm	6.50
	Dia. 160mm	7.50
Tea Pot Stand. Square With one crest	144mm sq	7.50
With crests and verse		15.25

Trinket Tray small 230mm

Square Teapot Stand

Tea Infuser and Lid

*Preserve Jar and Lid,
Strawberries*

*Circular Jar and Lid, Bees
and Clover*

Jam Dish or Nut Tray

Trinket Tray large 310mm

Circular Tea Pot Stand

*Oval Crinkle Tray Length
158mm*

Feeding Bowl

Scent Bottle with Stopper

Vase, Identical to Scent Bottle

		£ p
Tumblers or Beakers	(a) 40mm	3.00
	(b) 80mm	4.75
	(c) 95mm	5.50
	(d) 115mm	7.00
	(e) 145mm	8.25

Note: Some of (b), (c) and (d) varieties are occasionally found
with handles – same price.

Tumbler or Beaker – Barrel shaped	72mm	7.25
Octagonal Bowl	128mm across	10.00
Serviette Ring	40mm	7.50
Spoon Coat-of-arms in bowl	Length 150mm	75.00

Strawberry Dishes. Oval, decorated with strawberries

	Various sizes up to: Length 280mm	52.50
Tall Pepper Castor – PEPPER in blue	87mm	8.75
Tall Salt Castor – SALT in blue	87mm	8.75
	110mm	8.75
Tall Sugar Castor – SUGAR in blue	115mm	10.50
Tankard Mug with rim	70mm	4.75
Tankard Mug no rim	75mm	4.75
Tea Infuser and Lid	Dia. 82mm Height 35mm	10.00

Rectangular Stamp Box and Lid

Lip Salve Pot and Lid, Ball

Lip Salve Pot and Lid, Cylinder

Pomade Box and Lid

Puff Box and Lid

Hairpin Box

Pin Tray on Three Coral Legs

Crinkle Edge Pin Tray

Round Dish Plain Rim

Round Dish, with Turned Under Rim

Square Pintray, Plain

Square Pintray with Tassels

154

B.   Useful Articles

£ p

Trinket Set: Illustrated Galpin page 63, comprising:

			£ p
Trinket or Brush Tray (a) One crest	Length 310mm		17.50
(b) Multi-crested			35.00
(a) One crest	Length 230mm		13.00
(b) Multi-crested			26.00
Oval 'Crinkle' Tray	Length 158mm		5.50
Scent Bottle	130mm		8.50
Add £5.00 for stopper			
Hair Tidy – with HAIR TIDY **in blue and either**			
forget-me-nots or pink roses on lid	Dia. 70mm	Height 93mm	8.75
	Dia. 80mm	Height 93mm	13.00
Hat-Pin Stand	92mm		11.00
Powder Bowl and Lid. Large with shaped knob on lid.			
Often found in lustre	Dia. 130mm	Height 100mm	17.50
Puff Box and Lid	Dia. 82mm	Height 40mm	4.50
Pomade Box and Lid with small Knob on lid			
	Dia. 62mm	Height 40mm	4.50
Rectangular Box with forget-me-nots in relief on lid			
(a) Glazed	Length 98mm Width 52mm	Height 35mm	8.75
(b) Unglazed			13.00
(c) Word 'HAIRPINS'			17.50
(d) Illustrated Hairpins			24.50
Ring Tree	62mm		15.00
Lip-Salve Box – Ball	Dia. 43mm	Height 33mm	4.50
Lip-Salve Pot – Cylinder	Dia. 43mm	Height 35mm	4.00
Stamp Box, Rectangular			
	Length 40mm Width 52mm	Height 18mm	4.50

**HOLY WATER BOWL, used in a travelling communion
set, with IHS in red Gothic lettering on the side**

Dia. 52mm   15.00

Scallop Shell on Coral Ring

Limpet Shell, Orange Coral Legs

Scallop Shell 76mm on Three Short Legs

Pincushion

Circular Ash Tray

Safety Inkwell

Matchbox Holder

Match Holder

Shaving Mug

Pipe Tray

Candlestick, Column 153mm

Candle Bracket

156

£ p

PIN TRAYS:

			£ p
Round, Crinkle Dish		Dia. 70mm	3.50
Sometimes found with coral legs		75mm	3.50
when £7.50 should be added		85mm	4.00
		95mm	4.00
		100mm	4.50
Round Dish. Plain rim		Dia. 78mm	4.00

Round Dish. Heavy, with turned-under rim,
   usually early   Dia. 82mm   5.00

Limpet Shell, coral legs	Dia. 74mm	Height 36mm	8.25
Scallop Shell.	No legs	Length 140mm	10.50
	3 short legs	Length 140mm	10.50
	3 short legs	Length 101mm	7.00
	3 short legs	Length 76mm	5.50
	on coral legs	Length 76mm	10.50
	on coral ring	Length 76mm	20.00

Pin Cushion. Small, squat, wide vase with circular hole in
   centre to receive sawdust filling and velvet cover   Dia. 78mm   9.50

Square Tray. Plain   70mm sq   4.00
   See also Miniatures chapter

Square Tray. Heavy, with gilded tassel corners   70mm sq   5.50

CANDLE HOLDERS

Candle-Stick. Column		153mm	15.00
		127mm	15.00
		89mm	8.75

Candle-Holder. Flat, round, frilled, with handle   length 106mm   10.00

Candle-Holder. Flat, oval, frilled, with handle   (a) Length 120mm   10.00
   as above with standing Lincoln Imp on sconce   (b) Height 45mm   50.00

Candle-Holder. Flat, oval, frilled, with handle and
   Extinguisher   Length 170mm   24.50

Candle Bracket. (To hang on wall)   Height 170mm   22.50

CANDLE SNUFFERS

Cone	53mm	4.50
Mitre	60mm	55.00
Monk	82mm	130.00
Nun	94mm	175.00

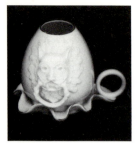

Durham Abbey Knocker
Nightlight

Mary Queen of Scots
Nightlight

Nightlight

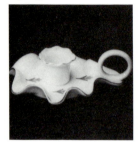

Candle Holder, Round,
Frilled with Handle

Candle Holder with Lincoln
Imp

Extinguisher Holder & Snuffer
Round, Frilled with Handle

Mitre Candle Snugger

Monk Candle Snuffer

Nun Candle Snuffer

Mr. Punch Candle Snuffer

Conical Shell Candle Snuffer

Welsh Lady Candle Snuffer

			£ p
Mr. Punch		92mm	40.00
Conical Shell		81mm	55.00
Welsh Lady	(a) White glazed	95mm	40.00
	(b) Multi-coloured	95mm	52.50
Extinguisher Stand, On round crinkle dish			7.50
Extinguisher Stand, Flat, round, frilled, with handle		Length 106mm	7.50

MISCELLANEOUS

Ashtray with coloured map of the Isle of Wight standing on rear edge of the ribbed dish			45.00
Ashtray. Circular, ribbed edge		Dia. 115mm	12.50
Ashtray. Oval with rests at each end and four thistle sprays in relief		Length 100mm	20.00
Inkwell, crinkle top, glazed		76mm	10.00
Inkwell, safety, tapered sides		57mm	8.50
Match Holder, unglazed		67mm	7.00
		76mm	9.50
Match-box Holder	Height 46mm	Length 66mm	30.00
Match-box. With lid – 'MATCHES'	Length 98mm	Width 52mm	20.00
Menu Holder		69mm	13.00
Moustache Cup and Saucer		98mm	22.50
Night-light. Base and Globe (In two parts.)	Length 105mm	Height 80mm	65.00

For **Durham Abbey Knocker** and **Mary Queen of Scots Night-lights** see Named Models Chapter.

Pipe-tray		Length 112mm	6.50
Shaving Mug		99mm	36.50
Slipper. To hang on wall as posy vase		Length 96mm	5.00
Tobacco Jars	(a) 8ozs. with lid	172mm	16.50
	(b) 3ozs. with lid	108mm	15.00

£ p

C. Ornamental Articles

FAIRY SIZES 50mm HIGH OR LESS:

Bag Vase		45mm	5.00
Ball Vase		46mm	4.00
		50mm	4.00
Bowl. Shallow		28mm	3.50
Cylinder Vase with three small feet		40mm	3.00
Early Squat Vase		40mm	4.00
Early Wide Taper Vase		45mm	5.00
Taper Vase Curved Base		45mm	5.00
		50mm	5.00
Pot-pourri Bowl. Small	Dia. 98mm	Height 40mm	8.50
Miniature Cheese Dish and Cover	Length 80mm	Height 50mm	16.00

OVER 50mm AND UP TO AND INCLUDING 75mm HIGH:

Amphora Vase with 2 butterfly handles	70mm	20.00
Bag Vase with white, green or blue cord	70mm	8.50
Ball Vase	71mm	7.50
	55mm	6.00
Ball Vase. With 2 handles	57mm	6.00
Ball Vase. With 3 handles	57mm	6.50
Bass Basket. Small	64mm	8.50
Club Vase	56mm	3.00
Cone Vase	56mm	3.00
Crinkle Vase. Conical. Flat base	71mm	4.50
Crinkle Vase. Conical. Rounded base	70mm	4.50
High-Lipped Ewer	72mm	3.50

		£ p
Jar. With decoration in relief. Sometimes called Ali-Baba Vase	57mm	3.50
Narrow Taper Vase	75mm	4.50
Thistle Vase. Two handles	64mm	4.50
Trumpet-top Vase. Two handles	75mm	4.50
Squat Taper Vase	64mm	4.50
Urn with or without handle	69mm	4.50
Wide Taper Vase, Early, everted rim, narrow neck	65mm	4.50
Wide Taper Vase, everted rim, wide neck	73mm	4.50

OVER 75mm AND UP TO AND INCLUDING 100mm HIGH:

Amphora Jar	80mm	8.75
Amphora Vase with three butterfly handles	85mm	22.50
Amphora Vase mounted on three Blue Balls and Plinth	93mm	13.00
Amphora Vase on blue or orange coral feet	85mm	13.00
Amphora Vase on 3 coral feet, with 3 butterfly handles	85mm	22.50
Bag Vase. Narrow	93mm	14.50
Bag Vase. Round	97mm	14.50
Ball Vase. With two handles	76mm	8.00
Ball Vase. With three handles	76mm	8.50
Bass Basket	80mm	8.00
	94mm	20.00

The smallest 64mm size has 'pinched in' sides at the centre of the top edges. The largest size is early and carries no arms.

Diamond-mouthed Vase	81mm	4.00
Diamond Vase. Old pattern, with 'foot'	79mm	8.75
Double Fern Pot. Flower pot in circular base to hold water	90mm	10.00

Ball Vase, Crinkle Top

Conical Crinkle Vase, Flat Base

Conical Crinkle Vase, Rounded Base

Thistle Vase, Two Handles

Trumpet Top Vase, Two Handles

Bagware Vase 70mm

Narrow Taper Vase with Everted Rim

Wide Taper Vase with Everted Rim

Urn with Handle 69mm

Pot-pourri Bowl small 41mm

Urn 70mm

Bag Vase Narrow

162

Taper Fern Pot on Base

Bass Basket small 64 mm

Bass Basket Medium 80mm

Bag Vase

Frilled Bowl

Cylinder Vase, Three Tiny Feet

Early Squat Vase 43mm

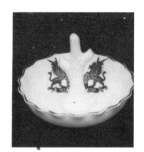

Ring Tree

High Lipped Ewer

Club Vase 56mm

Cone Vase 56mm

Jar with Decoration in Relief 57mm

		£ p
Egg-shaped Vase	80mm	5.00
Egg-shaped Vase with crinkle top	80mm	5.00
Egg-shaped Vase. With crinkle top and two blue butterfly handles	88mm	40.00
Jar	86mm	5.00
Early Lozenge-shaped Vase. With moulded bows at neck. Oval top	86mm	25.00
Pot-pourri Bowl or Rose Bowl. Large.		
(a) With rim around centre and no decoration	80mm	16.00
(b) Without rim and having a colourful star decoration on top	80mm	13.00
Scallop Edge Fern Pot	92mm	13.00
Taper Fern Pot on flat circular base Height 90mm Dia. 76mm		9.50
Taper Vase, rounded base	83mm	5.50
Thistle Vase with pineapple moulding in relief	79mm	4.75
Urn	96mm	5.25
OVER 100mm HIGH:		
Amphora Vase. With two or three butterfly handles	120mm	40.00
Ball Vase	114mm	11.00
Ball Vase. With four handles	118mm	17.50
Bass Basket, no crest	120mm	20.00
Club Specimen Vase	114mm	4.00
Cone Specimen Vase	117mm	4.00
Four Ball Group	114mm	65.00
	146mm	75.00
Globe Vase, narrow neck	196mm	26.00
Globe Vase. With two small knurled handles, narrow neck	196mm	30.00

Amphora Vase mounted on three Blue Balls and plinth

Amphora on Three Coral Feet

Amphora with Three Butterfly Handles

Ball Vase Two Handles

Ball Vase Three Handles

Jar 86mm

Egg-shaped Vase

Egg-shaped Vase, Crinkle Top 80mm

Scallop Edge Fern Pot

Pot-pourri Bowl, large 80mm

Taper Vase Rounded Base

Thistle (Vase) 80mm

		£ p
Globe Vase. With 3 small knurled handles, narrow neck	196mm	30.00
Goblet with central stem	162mm	26.00
Jar	109mm	7.50
Early Lozenge-shaped Vase. Upright with diamond top	139mm	30.00
Pear Shaped Vase. Flat with rectangular top	106mm	13.00
	122mm	17.50
	130mm	21.50
As above but with red or green grapevine decoration and sepia transfer of Windsor or Balmoral Castle	130mm	175.00
Pompeian Centrepiece On Plinth (Illustrated. Goss Record. 8th Edition: Pages 4 and 75)	125mm	24.50
	340mm	157.00
Pompeian Centrepiece. No plinth.	111mm	26.00
Quadruple Amphora Group. On plinth	150mm	63.50
Sack. Bagware	110mm	21.75
Taper Jar	110mm	8.75
Taper Vase. Crinkle top	170mm	11.00
Taper Vase. Crinkle top. With two blue angular handles and blue cord around neck	115mm	26.00
Taper Vase. With two high angular handles and fluted, everted rim	172mm	19.50
Triple Amphora. Three joined vases	110mm	26.50
Triple Bag Centrepiece (Goss Record. 8th Edition: Page 4) **With four oval bag vases, central one elongated**	190mm	100.00
Triple Bag and Shell Centrepiece. Having 3 glazed 66mm bag vases fixed together with a cone-shaped shell held centrally	159mm	100.00
Vase. Bell-shaped on socle base. Rare	203mm	40.00
Vase. Bulbous. With cup top and strap handle	176mm	17.50
	218mm	20.00

Diamond Mouthed Vase 80mm

Ball Vase, Crinkle Top

Ball Vase Four Handles

Clup Specimen Vase 114mm

Cone Specimen Vase 117mm

Early Lozenge Vase, Oval Top

Goblet 162mm

Early Lozenge-shaped Vase, Upright with Diamond Top

Jar 109mm

Pompeian Centre Piece 125mm

Pompeian Centre Piece 340mm

Four Ball Group

		£ p
Vase. With cup top and two strap handles	218mm	20.00
Vase, globular with two high handles and circular mouth	200mm	24.75
Early Vase. Round, flat faced, turquoise or plain leaves on border, oval base and mouth	120mm	52.50
Early Vase. Round, flat faced, wreath surround, rectangular base and round mouth	107mm	52.50
Early Vase. Oval, flat faced, wreath surround, rectangular base and oval mouth	170mm	60.00

MISCELLANEOUS ITEMS:

Holy Water Stoups:

These are found in 5 sizes, normally carrying the letters I.H.S. in red at the centre of the cross. Some examples carry normal coats-of-arms. The design comprises a shell-type water container surmounted by a cross pierced for wall-mounting.

	Height	*With any arms* £ p	*With I.H.S.* £ p
(a)	124mm	20.00	30.00
(b)	142mm	22.50	35.00
(c)	190mm	25.00	36.50
(d)	219mm	26.50	37.50
(e)	256mm	30.00	40.00

Salt Vase & Pestle. In Gothic script on 55mm club vase.

Mortar. Un-named Roman Mortarium with inscription on base in handwriting of W.H. Goss extolling the virtues of cleaning the teeth with ground salt   Dia. 95mm   Priced as a pair   75.00

Scarborough Flags Plate. Specially shaped plate made for the Southport Agent, J.G. Nairn   Width 105mm   265.00

Large Candleholder and Snuffer

Taper Vase, Curved Base

Taper Vase, Curved Base

Vase with Two Butterfly Handles

Circular Disc

Early 94mm Bass Basket

Lare Bagware Sack Vase

Early Vase, Flatfaced, Oval Mouth

Globe Vase with Three Small Knurled Handles, Narrow Neck

Quadruple Amphora Group on Plinth

Triple Bag and Shell Centrepiece

Taper Beaker with Handle

£ p

WALL POCKETS OR POSY HOLDERS

(a)	60mm	4.00
(b)	75mm	4.75
(c)	80mm	5.50
(d)	92mm	6.50
(e)	101mm	7.50
Usually named 'Flowerholder' or 'Hair Tidy' (f)	122mm	10.00
With arms other than below (g)	173mm	25.00

Wallpockets or Posy Holders. With arms of Cambridge
University or Eton College fully covering piece   173mm   40.00
(Goss Record. 8th Ed. Page 4)

Pear Shaped Vase

Triple Amphora

Taper Vase, Crinkle Top, 2 Blue Handles 107mm

Taper Vase, 2 High Handles 172mm

Vase, Bell-shaped on Socle Base 203mm

Bulbous Vase with Cup Top and Strap Handle

Early Round Flat Faced Vase, Oval Mouth 120mm

Early Round Flat Faced Vase, Rectangular Base, Round Top

Large Vase with Two Curved Handles

Holy Water Stoup

Scarborough Three-quarter Plate

W.H. Goss Face in Relief on Loving Cup

£ p

D. Loving Cups and Mugs

Loving Cups – Three handled:
See also Chapter headed POSTCARDS

(a)	38mm	8.00
(b)	43mm	7.50
(c)	51mm	7.50
(d)	57mm	8.50
(e)	76mm	11.00
(f)	83mm	12.50
(g)	95mm	13.00
(h)	121mm	30.00
(i)	133mm	50.00
Covered with separate lid (j)	133mm	75.00

NOTE: As a variation, some of the above may have square
handles

Mugs – two handled:

(a)	38mm	4.00
(b)	51mm	5.00
(c)	57mm	5.50
(d)	76mm	6.50
(e)	82mm	8.75
(f)	121mm	21.50

NOTE: As a variation, some of the above may have square
handles

Mugs – One handled:

(a)	38mm	3.00
(b)	51mm	3.50
(c)	57mm	4.00
(d)	76mm	6.00
(e)	82mm	6.50
(f)	121mm	17.50

NOTE: As a variation, some of the above may have square
handles

Mug, Barrel-shaped, one square handle.   74mm   9.00

N.B. See note on Minor Variations in Size. The items on this
page vary considerably in size and the nearest height should
be taken.

Wall Pocket

Flower Holder or Hair Tidy

Largest Wall Pocket 173mm

One Handle Mug 62mm

Mug Two Square Handles 76mm

Loving Cup Three Handles

Loving Cup Three Square Handles

Mug Two Handles

Brass Pipe Rack

Copper and Porcelain Dish Dia. 110mm

Brass Holder Containing Posy Vase

Goss Plated Spoon

£ p

DECORATIONS IN HIGH OR LOW RELIEF:

The following may be found on two or three-handled loving cups

In high relief **W.H. Goss**		110mm	75.00

Usually also bearing the arms of W.H. Goss and
 Stoke-on-Trent.
 In low relief –
 Profiles of:

King Edward VII	two handled	90mm	75.00
King Edward VII	three handled	90mm	85.00
King Edward VII	three handled	120mm	110.00
King George V	two handled	90mm	85.00
King George V	three handled	120mm	110.00

These are usually found with their corresponding
 commemorative devices.

Lincoln Imp – In high relief on a Beaker	80mm	50.00

Flower Holder with profile of Shakespeare in low relief.		
Glazed	122mm	100.00

The following Loving Cups may also be found, and details are
 given in the Named Models and Special Shapes Chapter:
 Durham Abbey Knocker
 Mary, Queen of Scots
 Stratford Sanctuary Knocker

Metalware

A metal teaspoon was produced with the permission of W.H. Goss, bearing the name 'Goss' in the bowl, and having a handle in the shape of the Portland Vase. On this Portland Vase was an enamelled coat-of-arms, usually that of London, but several others are known.

One example has the word 'SILVER' clearly impressed into the shaft but the base metal is obviously nickel-silver, which takes on a dull yellowish hue unless kept regularly polished. Presumably these spoons were originally silver-plated, but time and wear have resulted in many losing their plating to some extent.

Production of these spoons is estimated to have taken place from about 1910 until the mid-1920s, and they were made in Birmingham by the firm of Arbuckle (no longer in existence). Arbuckles were large producers of such seaside souvenirs, and the 'Goss' spoons would only have represented a very small portion of the firm's total output.

Length of Spoon 120mm   £30.00
See also Domestic and Ornamental Wares (A) for porcelain spoon.

A Pipe-rack, a Posy Vase holder and a Mantel Clock, all carrying Goss porcelain inserts, (usually bearing arms commemorating Queen Victoria's Diamond Jubilee, not of a design found elsewhere on Goss china), but made of Brass, can be found. The brass manufacturer was Harcourt, and a registered number of 128998 is quoted, which indicates a date of 1889. Possibly Harcourts were anticipating the Golden Jubilee, but there are probably other examples with normal coats-of-arms. (NOTE: it is necessary to dismantle these items to find the 'Gosshawk/W.H. Goss' mark. Sometimes the corners of the plaque have been trimmed to fit the brass holder by the manufacturer).

Price range £75.00–£100.00

There are two other Goss items which have metal surrounds. In each case they have flat circular porcelain bases and raised (a) copper and (b) silver rims fitted to them, converting them to a variety of ash or pin trays.

The copper-mounted piece bears the four-flag wartime decoration, while the silver rimmed dish carries a coat-of-arms.

Diameter of porcelain portion of copper dish 70mm
Diameter 104mm   £15.00
Silver rim dish   £22.50

Parian Ware

A. Busts

Busts were made virtually throughout the whole existence of the firm commencing around 1860. Early busts normally had a round (or socle) plinth, and were often of classical rather than political or literary figures.

The main series of busts made by the factory seems to have commenced in the mid 1870s and ended in 1906 with the bust of W.H. Goss himself – a fitting memorial to a fine line of Royalty, writers, politicians, and noble men and women. The main series were almost all made with the well-known square two-step plinth although there were several exceptions, such as the 'Scottish' busts and certain of the larger busts which had a combination of socle-on-octagonal plinths. The square plinth would normally carry the name of the person on its lower step, but this is not universal, and names are often found extending over both steps – or impressed into the back of the bust.

The glazing of certain busts has given rise to speculation as to whether this was by way of experiment or by demand. It is felt that probably the former was the case, and the period of the experiment appears to be for a few years either side of 1900. In the following listing, busts will be assumed to be unglazed, and to have square two-step plinths, unless otherwise indicated.

Queen Victoria
Socle/Octagonal Plinth

Queen Victoria wearing Mob
Cap

Queen Victoria Wearing
Crown

Prince of Wales

The Princess of Wales

King Edward VII

King Edward VII, Socle
Plinth

Queen Alexandra, Socle
Plinth

Keystone of the
Kingdom, Lord Beaconsfield

The Prince of Wales

The Prince of Wales,
Reverse

Keystone of the
Kingdom, Lord Derby

ROYALTY

Queen Victoria in Mob-cap, socle/octagonal plinth	236mm	275.00
	201mm	150.00
Queen Victoria in Mob-cap	151mm	100.00
	Glazed 129mm	90.00
	Unglazed 129mm	90.00
	101mm	80.00

Queen Victoria – wearing Imperial Crown, the top of which is
extremely fragile   approx. 172mm   175.00

Note: Should any of the above busts bear reference on the back
to Queen Victoria's Diamond Jubilee, it will indicate that
they are commemorative items and of higher value, say,
£15.00 extra.
Some busts of Queen Victoria have a simple frill to the front
of the bonnet, others have a double frill and some may be
found with either. Value unchanged.

Prince of Wales later King Edward VII wearing Masonic collar	520mm	1250.00
Prince of Wales later King Edward VII	167mm	135.00
Princess of Wales later Queen Alexandra	176mm	135.00
King Edward VII	163mm	135.00
King Edward VII socle plinth	glazed 133mm	125.00
	unglazed 133mm	125.00
Queen Alexandra socle plinth	132mm	125.00
Queen Alexandra	approx. 175mm	150.00
Prince of Wales, later King Edward VIII, bearing details of Investiture, and mounted on column bearing arms	143mm	160.00
As above but lacking Investiture details	143mm	125.00

OTHER

Adonis socle plinth	265mm	400.00
Apollo socle plinth – with some gilding	approx. 260mm	450.00
Beaconsfield	104mm	110.00
	154mm	100.00
	320mm	300.00

Beaconsfield

Beaconsfield, Socle Plinth

Beaconsfield Wearing Coronet

Burns Socle Plinth

Burns, Socle/Octagonal Plinth

The Beautiful Duchess

Beethoven

John Bright

John Bunyan

Byron

Byron Socle/Octagonal Plinth

Clytie

		£ p
Beaconsfield – wearing coronet	181mm	175.00
Beaconsfield socle plinth, glazed	111mm	100.00
Beautiful Duchess, The. White, on 3-step plinth	242mm	700.00
Coloured, on 3-step plinth.		
Almost certainly the Duchess of Devonshire	242mm	1000.00
NOTE: This bust stands on a separate highly ornate plinth, always unmarked. Height 132mm. Add the price of this plinth to that of the bust when present		200.00
Beethoven	glazed 116mm	125.00
	unglazed 116mm	125.00
Bright	glazed 165mm	125.00
	unglazed 165mm	125.00
Bunyan	glazed 132mm	125.00
	unglazed 132mm	125.00
Burns socle plinth	glazed 136mm	100.00
	unglazed 136mm	100.00
	155mm	100.00
Burns socle/octagonal plinth	glazed 166mm	125.00
	unglazed 166mm	125.00
Byron	179mm	135.00
Byron socle/octagonal plinth	193mm	150.00
Christ socle plinth		400.00
Classical Lady, coloured, with butterfly upon lapel. Socle/octagonal plinth. A similar bust was made by Belleek, evidently after the Goss original	270mm	400.00
Clytie socle plinth	215mm	250.00
Clytie square base	approx. 160mm	150.00
Derby socle plinth	105mm	110.00
Derby square base	105mm	110.00
Derby	glazed 160mm	100.00
	unglazed 160mm	100.00

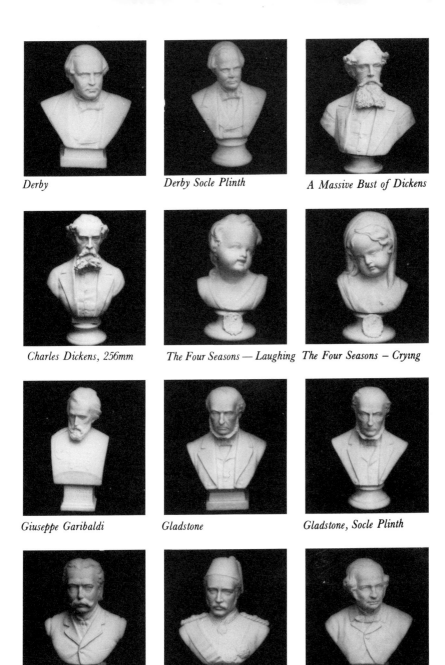

Derby

Derby Socle Plinth

A Massive Bust of Dickens

Charles Dickens, 256mm

The Four Seasons — Laughing

The Four Seasons – Crying

Giuseppe Garibaldi

Gladstone

Gladstone, Socle Plinth

W.H. Goss

General Gordon

Granville

W.C. Gully

S.C. Hall

Handel

Hartington

Georgiana Jewitt

Llewellyn Jewitt

Mary Queen of Scots

Ann Hathaway, Coloured

Ann Hathaway

Longfellow

Sir Wilfrid Lawson

Mars

		£ p
Dickens socle plinth	256mm	200.00
Dickens socle plinth – Goss & Peake	650mm	1250.00

Four Seasons – Busts of two children

(a) Laughing	218mm	165.00
(b) Crying and wearing shawl on head	225mm	165.00

		£ p
Gladstone square base	approx. 400mm	300.00
Gladstone	162mm	125.00
Gladstone socle plinth	132mm	110.00

Lady Godiva
(Goss Record. 9th Edition: Page 29)

(a)	White	108mm	70.00
(b)	Coloured	108mm	145.00

		£ p
Guiseppe Garibaldi	174mm	350.00
Gordon, General	189mm	125.00
Goss, William Henry	glazed 160mm	110.00
	unglazed 160mm	100.00
Granville	glazed 176mm	125.00
	unglazed 176mm	125.00
Gully, W.C.	120mm	175.00
Hall, S.C. socle plinth	376mm	1000.00
Handel	glazed 116mm	125.00
	unglazed 116mm	125.00
Hartington	glazed 174mm	125.00
	unglazed 174mm	125.00
Hartington socle plinth	130mm	150.00

Hathaway, Ann
(Goss Record. 9th Edition:
Page 30, on two books)

(a)	White	75mm	60.00
(b)	White	100mm	65.00
(c)	Coloured	100mm	165.00

		£ p
Irving, Washington	400mm	400.00

Milton

Milton, Socle Base

Thomas Moore

Sir Moses Montefiore with Hat

Sir Moses Montefiore without Hat

Mozart

Napoleon

Palmerston, Socle Base

Palmerston, Socle Base 223mm

Lord Palmerston on Socle Base and Fluted Column

Lady Godiva, White

Peeping Tom, White

		£	p

Jewitt, Georgiana socle/octagonal plinth — 198mm — 750.00

The inscription on the back of this bust reads: *"Georgiana. The beloved
wife of Edwin A.G. Jewitt, and daughter of William H. Goss. She was
born in London July 30, 1855, died at Matlock, Nov. 3, 1889 and is buried
in Winster Churchyard".*

The grave may still be seen today in the delightful Derbyshire village of
Winster.

Jewitt, Llewellyn socle plinth — 380mm — 750.00

The inscription on the back of this bust reads:
*This bust of Llewellyn Jewitt F.S.A. is made expressly for presentation to
his son Mr. Edwin Augustus George Jewitt on the occasion of his 21st
birthday the 13th Oct. 1879 as a mark of the highest esteem for both by
their devoted friend William Henry Goss.*

Dr. Samuel Johnson socle/octagonal plinth — 190mm — 325.00

Keystones of the Kingdom, The, being virtually life-size heads
of **(a) Lord Derby** — 300.00
    (b) William Gladstone — 300.00

Mounted on 'Keystone' shaped slabs dated 1880
Dimensions: Height 300mm; Width 175mm reducing to 144mm
See also Terra-cotta chapter.

Lawson, Sir Wilfrid — 163mm — 300.00

Longfellow — 174mm — 175.00

Mars socle plinth — 320mm — 400.00

Mary, Queen of Scots socle plinth — 131mm — 150.00

Mendelssohn — glazed 116mm — 125.00
    unglazed 116mm — 125.00

Milton — glazed 167mm — 125.00
    unglazed 167mm — 125.00

Milton socle plinth — 210mm — 110.00

Montefiore, sometimes **Montifiore, Sir Moses** with hat — 130mm — 135.00

Montefiore, Sir Moses without hat — 123mm — 145.00

Moore, Thomas — 170mm — 150.00

Mozart — glazed 118mm — 125.00
    unglazed 118mm — 125.00

			£ p
Napoleon	square tapered plinth, unglazed	142mm	50.00
	plinth only glazed	142mm	50.00
	completely glazed	142mm	50.00

NOTE: This bust normally carries the arms of St. Helena, and the
above prices are for this model. Rare specimens have been found
bearing the arms of Napoleon, which would increase the above
values by £20.00

Northcote, Sir S.	glazed	169mm	125.00
	unglazed	169mm	125.00

Ophelia socle plinth	approx.	225mm	400.00

Palmerston socle plinth		164mm	100.00
		223mm	100.00

Palmerston socle plinth and fluted column		335mm	110.00

Peeping Tom

(Goss Record. 9th Edition:	(a) White glazed	114mm	70.00
Pages 29 & 30)	(b) White unglazed	114mm	70.00
	(c) Coloured	114mm	125.00

Pitman, Sir Isaac. This bust is an apparent anomaly. Sculpted by
T. Brock, R.A. in London in 1887, it has an unusual square
plinth, and carries the 'Goss England' mark. In view of its early
date it is included in this section. 281mm 400.00

Punch, Mr. 295mm 450.00
The three-quarter length figure resting on a base consisting of
four volumes of Punch and backed by two more. Copyright 1861

Salisbury	glazed	163mm	125.00
	unglazed	163mm	125.00

Scott, Sir Walter	glazed	176mm	125.00
	unglazed	176mm	125.00

Scott, Sir Walter socle plinth, and wearing tartan plaid	135mm	30.00

Scott, Sir Walter socle plinth, and wearing jacket, waistcoat
and cravat 138mm 100.00

Scott, Sir Walter socle/octagonal plinth, and wearing jacket,
waistcoat and cravat 168mm 175.00

Shakespeare from the monument, socle/octagonal plinth.
Impressed in manuscript 'Shakespeare from the monument at
Stratford-On-Avon. 1616'. coloured 165mm 125.00

Sir S. Northcote

Lady Godiva, Coloured

Peeping Tom, Coloured

Shakespeare,
Socle/Octagonal Plinth

Salisbury

Sir Walter Scott

Sir Walter Scott Wearing
Jacket and Cravat

Sir Walter Scott, Tartan
Plaid

Sir Isaac Pitman

Shakespeare from
Monument, Coloured

The Chandos
Shakespeare

Shakespeare Socle Plinth

£　p

Shakespeare from tomb mounted upon two books
(Goss Record. 9th Edition: Page 30)

(a) White	75mm	50.00
(b) White	102mm	30.00
(c) Coloured	102mm	55.00
(d) White	158mm	50.00
(e) Coloured	158mm	80.00
(f) Black	158mm	70.00
(g) White	200mm	75.00
(h) Coloured	200mm	100.00

Shakespeare – The Chandos, socle plinth	133mm	100.00
Shakespeare – The Davenant	117mm	50.00
	165mm	65.00
Shakespeare socle plinth	224mm	65.00

See also GOSS ENGLAND chapter for late
example of a bust of Shakespeare.

Sister Dora	174mm	145.00
Southey	180mm	125.00
Southey socle/octagonal plinth	205mm	150.00
Stanley, H.M. socle/octagonal plinth	212mm	300.00
Swain, Charles socle plinth	283mm	500.00
Veiled Bride, The, after Monti, socle plinth	270mm	400.00
Venus de Milo socle plinth	273mm	400.00
Virgin Mary socle plinth		200.00
Wallace, Sir William socle plinth	134mm	175.00
Webb, Captain Matthew	230mm	400.00
Wesley	unglazed 168mm	125.00
	glazed 168mm	125.00

NOTE: It would appear that Black Basalt busts of Wesley were
also made, height 154mm – but these, whilst being perfect,
smaller replicas of the above, carry no manufacturer's
identification mark. The author however, believes them to be
products of the Goss factory. Same price.

Wordsworth	164mm	90.00

Sister Dora

Southey

Southey,
Socle/Octagonal Plinth

Charles Swain

Sir William Wallace

H.M. Stanley

Wordsworth

The Veiled Bride

Venus de Milo

John Wesley

Virgin Mary

Black Bust of Wesley

B. Figures and Groups

£ p

Attempting to list the large numbers of Goss figures is difficult.
Certain figures are sufficiently distinctive to identify by
description, and are of known subjects. But there are many,
varying in height between 200mm and 450mm which defy
accurate description. The more readily identifiable items are
listed here, but similar figures of the same heights will have
comparable values.

Angel, standing with hands clasped in front		318mm	250.00
Angel, holding shell in left hand		318mm	250.00
Angel, kneeling, holding large shell (stoup). Reputedly St. John's Font, Barmouth		148mm	300.00
Bather, nude, in pensive mood, seated on rock	approx.	220mm	275.00
Bather, nude, standing beside pump		410mm	650.00
Bear and Ragged Staff (Goss Record. 9th Edition: Page 31)			
(a) White unglazed		90mm	85.00
(b) White glazed with shield and arms			
(Add £25.00 for Warwick Arms)		90mm	85.00
(c) White unglazed but coloured harness, chain & base		90mm	170.00
(d) Brown and coloured, glazed		90mm	300.00
(e) Brown unglazed		90mm	220.00
Blind Beggar and Peasant Girl circular base		295mm	400.00
Boys – a pair			
(a) Holding paint palette		220mm	225.00
(b) Holding writing tablet		220mm	225.00
Bride of Abydos, The, Goss & Peake		535mm	1000.00
Two Cherubs			
(a) The Captive Cupid, some colouring, feet chained		215mm	300.00
(b) Cherub Standing, holding book		220mm	300.00
Child kneeling on cushion, at prayer			
(a) Coloured, the decoration is probably late.		165mm	400.00
(b) White, glazed or unglazed		165mm	300.00

Angel Holding Shell | Classical Figurine | Classical Figurine

Classical Figurine | Leda and the Swan | Lady Holding Kid

Bear and Ragged Staff | The Bride of Abydos | Ophelia

The Boot-black | The Crossing Sweeper | Devil Looking Over Lincoln

191

£ p

Children – a pair
   (a) Bootblack   210mm   325.00
   (b) Crossing-sweeper   224mm   325.00
NOTE: This pair, originally published in 1873 as unglazed figures
   were re-issued in the latter days of the firm, but in full colour. In
   the earlier models, the Post Box has a loose top, while in the later
   models, it is fixed.
   (a) Bootblack, coloured   210mm   650.00
   (b) Crossing-sweeper, coloured   224mm   650.00

Chimney Sweep, Boy, coloured, decoration probably late.   292mm   750.00

Classical Figurine, Comedy, lady holding mask away from
   face   320mm   250.00

Classical Figurine, Tragedy, lady with dagger. White or with
   some colour   328mm   250.00

Classical Ladies, A pair, each reclining on large base,
   one observant, the other in pensive mood   each   350mm   300.00

Cleopatra, seated on draped tree stump holding aloft an asp.
   On oval base   240mm   350.00

Cupid, asleep lying on a bed with bow and arrow.   270mm ×140mm   400.00

Cuthbert of Durham, St.   134mm   400.00
(Goss Record. 9th Edition: Page 15)

Devil Looking Over Lincoln, The
                      (a) White   147mm   50.00
                      (b) Brown   147mm   75.00

Figurine, standing in pensive mood with hand under chin.
   Gown edged in gold   345mm   225.00

Figurine, standing, playing lyre. Some colouring   340mm   200.00

Figurines, a pair, each holding a baby.   each   375mm   250.00

Figurines, a pair, **'Seasons'** – gowns edged in gold
   (a) Holding sheaf of corn on head   345mm   225.00
   (b) Holding drape on head   345mm   225.00

Gordon, General. Standing on square base
   Not seen by the author   approx.   330mm   400.00

*Child, Partly Draped standing
with Foot on Stool*

Child Seated on Rock

*Partly Draped Bather Seated
on Rock*

*Cleopatra Holding an Asp
Aloft*

Classical Figurine

Classical Figurine

Classical Figurine — Tragedy

St. Cuthbert of Durham

Child Kneeling on a Cushion

Cherub Standing

*Winged Putto, the Captive
Cupid*

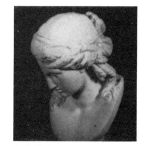

Ophelia?

£ p

Godiva, Lady, on horseback. Sometimes inscribed '*From the figure in Maidstone Museum, Maidstone*' (Goss Record. 9th Edition: Pages 29 & 30)

(a) White	112mm	225.00
(b) White	133mm	250.00
(c) White	165mm	300.00
(d) Coloured	182mm	600.00
(e) White	182mm	450.00

Goss, Evangeline. The child sleeping on a cushion, either forming the lid of a casket, white or coloured, or as a solid-based item (Illustrated in Goss Record. 8th Edition: Page 4. Bottom right.)

Length of child 130mm

(a) Coloured, on casket	350.00
(b) White, on casket	220.00
(c) White, on cushion	125.00
(d) Coloured, on cushion	200.00

Grecian Water Carrier, holding pitcher aloft, on circular base. 250mm   200.00

Happy and Unhappy Children, The. A pair of figures from originals by M. Simonis of Brussels, shown at the Great Exhibition of 1851
(a) Happy Child, holding toy 'Punch'   approx.   150mm   250.00
(b) Unhappy Child, having broken drum   143mm   250.00

Dr. Kenealy. The caricature head entitled **'Dewdrops'.**   130mm   125.00

Dr. Kenealy. Caricature Figure. Standing and holding top-hat and umbrella, as spill-vase and match-holder.   191mm   225.00

Dr Kenealy, depicted as a lion on circular plinth holding a shield 'Sir Roger Tichborne and Magna Charta Defended' Presumed to have been produced by W. H. Goss.   225.00

Lady, Holding Child, Playing Horn on oval base   275mm   600.00

Classical Figurine, holding a kid
(a) White   435mm   400.00
(b) Coloured   435mm   950.00

Leda and the Swan
(a) White   430mm   400.00
(b) Coloured   430mm   950.00
The above two figures are a pair.

Lady, with dove feeding from sea-shell   320mm   400.00

Lincoln Imp. In high relief on beakers. See DOMESTIC WARE D.

Lincoln Imp. Miniature version on sconce of frilled candle-holder. See DOMESTIC WARE B

Lady Godiva on Horseback

The Happy Child

Unhappy Child Length 143mm

Lady Godiva on Horseback, Coloured

Lincoln Imp

Lincoln Imp on Pedestal

Little Red Riding Hood

Shakespeare Leaning on a lectern

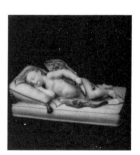

Cupid Lying on a Cushion Length 270mm

Bullock and Sheep Group

Bullock and Sheep Group, Reverse

Fox and its Prey

£   p

Lincoln Imp. (Goss Record. 9th Edition: Page 22)
To hang on wall.

(a) White	38mm	50.00
(b) White	78mm	25.00
(c) Brown	78mm	30.00
(d) White	106mm	30.00
(e) Brown	106mm	40.00
(f) White	120mm	40.00
(g) Brown	120mm	45.00
(h) White	145mm	45.00
(i) Brown	145mm	50.00

These pieces often appear unmarked. Whilst they are probably
from Goss moulds they cannot be properly considered as such
and are worth approximately £5.00.
NOTE: Some of the above models are also found glazed, usually
with Blackpool Arms for which about £10 should be deducted.

Lincoln Imp seated on column

(a) White unglazed	114mm	50.00
(b) White glazed plinth, usually with matching arms.	114mm	75.00
(c) Brown	114mm	150.00

Little Red Riding Hood	270mm	600.00
Ophelia.	535mm	1000.00
Goss & Peake		
Peasant Girl, circular base	225mm	275.00
Putti, a pair of seated cherubs each	200mm	250.00
Queen of Light, The. Some colouring	332mm	300.00

Shakespeare

Full length figure from monument in Westminster Abbey,	175mm	225.00
standing, leaning on a lectern.	143mm	165.00
Shepherd Boy. Circular plinth approx.	300mm	500.00
Trusty Servant, The	202mm	1250.00
William of Wykeham	202mm	1250.00

A Winchester pair in full colours. William carries a removable
crook with a wire stem without which the figure is incomplete.

Venus, emerging from between two large shells, supported by		
dolphins. Unglazed or part glazed	175mm	300.00
Young Woman Praying. Standing, possibly the Virgin Mary	275mm	250.00

Lady Holding Child Playing Horn

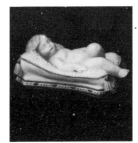

Evangeline Goss on a Cushion

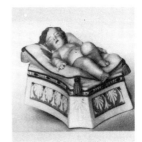

Evangeline Goss Lying on a Shaped Casket

Virgin Mary

Classical Lady, Observant, on Large Base

Classical Lady, in Pensive Mood, on Large Base

The Trusty Servant

William of Wykeham

Bird Resting on Edge of Nest

Bird on Tree Stump

Bird on Rock, Inkwell

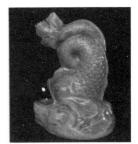

Dolphin Inkwell

C.   Ornamental Early Ware   £   p

Bird, a wren standing on the edge of a nest, coloured light blue
  inside   70mm   200.00

Bird on Tree Stump, as posy vase   approx.   100mm   125.00

Bird on a rock, as inkwell   125mm   150.00

Bird's Egg. Apart from the named Guillemot's Egg with a pointed
end, for which see NAMED MODELS Chapter, there is also a
similar-sized sea-bird egg with a rounded base. Both varieties were
produced in beige, blue and green speckled colourings.
  (a) Closed   93mm   50.00
  (b) Open, to hang as posy vase   83mm   50.00

Bird's Nest in Napkin
  (a) White glazed only   185mm   175.00
  (b) Forget-Me-Nots or arms   185mm   175.00

Bowl and Lid, circular. The body formed from pink rose petals
  trimmed with green leaves. The lid has a rosebud knop   Dia. 73mm   35.00

Brooches. These are many and varied, with some twenty different
designs, both white unglazed and coloured glazed. 'Initial'
brooches were made, with the appropriate letter on a
'criss-cross' white background, and surrounded by an oval
floral wreath, but these are rare. It is known that some coloured
brooches were being made as late as the mid-1920s.

  (a) White   45.00
  (b) Coloured   55.00
  (c) Initial   125.00

See also Floral Decorations

Bullock and Two Sheep on oval plinth   148mm   750.00

Comport, with three short legs.
  Floral decoration in relief inside bowl.   Dia.   234mm   100.00

Cream 'Leaf' Jug, two moulded leaves   100.00

Cream Jug and Sugar Bowl sea-urchin design.
  Jug 60mm Bowl diameter 100mm
  (a) White glazed   Each   30.00
  (b) Some turquoise colouring   Each   35.00

£   p

Cream Jug. Glazed, having acanthus leaf pattern in low relief.
Many variations of coloured decoration, both to handle and
body can be found, as well as inscriptions in Gothic script,
'A PRESENT FROM . . .' or 'FROM . . .'   75mm   30.00

Dog Bowl. Illuminated lettering in relief around rim.
'Quick at Work, Quick at Meals'   Dia.   210mm   100.00

Dolphin – Tail uppermost on small round hollow plinth,
presumably for use as posy holder or inkwell.   98mm   100.00
The example seen has an early purple Gosshawk mark without
lettering.

Elephant with Howdah
     (a) White glazed   153mm   500.00
     (b) Some colouring   153mm   750.00
     (c) Earthenware   160mm   500.00

for **EWER,** early see PARIAN C., VASES

Floral Decorations: Being similar to the porcelain portion of
coloured brooches, but fixed to the tops of powder-bowls, and
the sides of lozenge and other vases. Also used was a larger coloured
floral decoration, completely covering the top of a powder bowl.
Any of these decorations would increase the value of the item by
approximately: 50.00

See also Brooches.

Fox and Its Prey, a rooster, on oval plinth.
This study may be found in either Parian or Earthenware.   90mm   225.00

Fruit Basket. Glazed, with acanthus-leaf pattern and strap   Length
handle. Early.   224mm   150.00

Fruit Basket. Glazed, fluted with turquoise strap
handle.   Length   120mm   100.00

Fruit Basket. Glazed, Dutch style with turquoise
coral handle. See DOMESTIC WARE. A.

Hand. Glazed. Probably a ring tree.   93mm   45.00

Hand. Glazed, holding bag vase.
Some fine gilding and turquoise cord and button.   122mm   65.00

Lithophane (dated 1888) depicting lady with star in her
hair.   dia.   89mm   750.00

Early Lozenge Vase with Oval Mouth and Floral Decoration

White Floral Brooch

Coloured Floral Brooch

Coloured Powder Bowl with Floral Decoration

Powder Bowl and Lid with Floral Decoration

Rare Coloured Bowl and Lid with Floral Decoration

Late Floral Decoration

Dewdrops, Dr. Kenealy Spillholder

Dr. Kenealy Spill and Match Holder

Pin Cushion, Acanthus Leaf Pattern

Early Jug, Acanthus Leaf Pattern

Elephant with Howdah

£ p

Monmouth Masks.
(Goss Record. 9th Edition: Page 23)
Although there are actually three masks in Geoffrey
Monmouth's study: the Miller, the Knight, and the Angel, only
the former two have so far been found reproduced by Goss:

The Miller	(a) White glazed	81mm	157.00
	(b) White unglazed	81mm	175.00
	(c) Brown	81mm	265.00
	(d) White	95mm	200.00
	(e) Brown	95mm	265.00
	(f) White	120mm	200.00
	(g) Brown	120mm	265.00
The Knight	(a) White unglazed	80mm	157.00
	(b) Brown unglazed	96mm	265.00
	(c) Brown unglazed	115mm	265.00

Mushroom. Brown unglazed, with green grass
around base of stem   60mm   250.00

Oval Wall Plaques. A number of these were
produced with busts in low relief centrally. The
plaques were normally gold-edged with ribbon
ornamentation at the top. The title for each will
be found lightly impressed under the subject.

Oakley Coles	200mm	400.00
J.S. Crapper	200mm	400.00
Robert Garner	200mm	400.00
The Prince of Wales, later King Edward VII	200mm	400.00
Eugene Rimmel	200mm	400.00
Revd. Lovelace Stamer	200mm	400.00

These plaques are upright oval, but there is one which is
horizontal oval:

Child with Large Dog 'Can't You Talk?'   180mm   400.00

NOTE: All the above plaques would appear to have been
commissioned and published by J.S. Crapper, a colleague of
W.H. Goss. All plaques bear the impressed 'W.H. GOSS'
marks.

Pendant in Form of a Cross with ivy decoration in relief
Unglazed brown parian   80mm   150.00

Picture frame
containing sepia pictorial of Romsey Abbey Crucifix,
all made in one piece.   Height 170mm Width 137mm   130.00

Pierced Bowl.
(Illustrated Goss Record. 8th Edition: Page 4.   Dia. 140mm   100.00
Middle shelf)

Small Basket with Flutes and Strap

Basket with Coral Handle

Basket with Acanthus Leaves and Strap

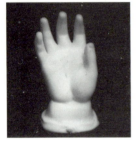

Hand Ring Tree

Lithophane

Pierced Dish 242mm

Monmonth Mask, The Miller

Monmouth Mask, The Knight

Rare Oval Plaque

Early Sheep

Hand Holding Bag Vase

Squirrel and Tree-trunk

Crucifix Pendant

Early Cup and Saucer with Raised Floral Decoration

Early Teapot with Raised Floral Decoration

Rare Early Flask with Cipher Under Crown

Leaf Pattern Cream Jug

Sark Mild Churn, Early

Rare Brown Mushroom

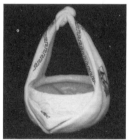

Bird's Nest in a Napkin

Bird's Nest in Napkin, Forget-me-nots

Lozenge Vase, Oval Mouth with Floral Decoration

Coloured Floral Brooch

Winchester Flagon

£ p

Pierced Dish in imitation basket-work, glazed and
having a coat-of-arms in base of dish, usually of
Boston.
Length
242mm   45.00

Pin-cushion. A round, glazed porcelain base with
shell pattern, to be filled with sawdust and top
covered in velvet. Inscribed in Gothic lettering
'A PRESENT FROM . . .'
Dia. 70mm   15.00

A Special Plaque. (Illustrated, Goss Record. 8th Edition:
Page 4, Top Shelf) measuring 335mm x 275mm was made,
possibly specially for the Exhibition at Stoke-on-Trent in
1913 on the occasion of Their Majesties' visit to the Potteries.
Only one specimen is known and the piece is believed to be
unique. It depicts two bulls fighting, is in low relief and
unglazed. The border is perfectly plain.
700.00

Plates. Circular. Various early unglazed plates, measuring
some 345mm in diameter were produced. Some were left
completely white while others had the wording, coats-of-
arms, or other decoration in colour. The most common is the
Winchester College plate, which often bears the inscription:
Published by W. SAVAGE on the back.

Arms of Winchester College centrally, with *Manners
Makyth Man* on surrounding rim:

(a)	White	100.00
(b)	Coloured	200.00

Arms of St. Cross Hospice, Winchester:

(a)	White unglazed	100.00
(b)	White or cream glazed	100.00
(c)	Coloured	200.00

Eat Thy Bread with Thankfulness

(a)	White	100.00
(b)	Coloured	200.00

Think, Thank and Thrive
(Illustrated. Goss Record. 8th Edition: Page 4)

(a)	White	100.00
(b)	Coloured	200.00

Holly Decoration Round Rim
hence known as a Christmas pudding plate

(a)	Coloured	348mm	150.00
(b)	White	348mm	100.00

Plate with glazed recessed centre and heavy relief decoration
around wide rim
Dia. 200mm   75.00

Oval Plaque 'J.S. Crapper'

Oval Plaque 'Oakley Coles'

Oval Plaque 'Robert Garner'

Oval Plaque 'Rev. Lovelace Stamer'

Oval Plaque 'The Prince of Wales'

Oval Plaque 'Can't You Talk?'

Oval Plaque 'Eugene Rimmel'

Wall Vase, Derby

Wall Vase, Disraeli (Beaconsfield)

Wall Vase, Granville

Wall Vase, Georgiana Jewitt

Wall Vase, Bright

£   p

Plate, circular, with gilded edge, magenta band, holly and
  mistletoe – and inscribed: *A MERRY CHRISTMAS*   Dia. 225mm   125.00

**Plate pierced, decorated in relief with linked chain
  decoration.** 'Bournemouth' coat-of-arms in centre. This
  is from the same mould as that used for the comport
  featured in the 1862 International Exhibition.   Dia. 234mm   40.00

A Specially Decorated Plate, one of only four produced in
  bagware. 150mm in diameter, with coloured cartoon of two
  doctors, Major Embleton and Major Goss. This was
  specially designed by Margaret Goss around 1920   150.00

Plate, pierced with pink band as decoration. The   Dia. 300mm
  body is earthenware and a matching comport was made.   Plate   75.00
This plate may also be found with an early transfer   Comport   75.00
of a child in the centre

Platters, Oval Bread, 310mm x 250mm which appear
  (a) unglazed, with coloured lettering and (b) glazed with
  plain or coloured lettering, and with arms or other motif
  central.
Where Reason Rules, The Appetite Obeys around rim.
Give Us This Day Our Daily Bread around rim.
  White or cream glazed.   Price range: 50.00–125.00

Platters, Almost Oval 328mm x 245mm carrying the *Think,*
  Thank and Thrive wording around the border are found with
  two differing types of lettering
  (a) White unglazed   100.00
  (b) With coloured lettering, glazed or unglazed   125.00

Posy Basket. Glazed.
  (Illustrated Goss Record. 8th Edition. Page 4, at bottom)   125mm   200.00

Posy or Cluster of Flowers. Various, coloured in 'Crown
  Staffordshire' style   approx. 70mm   75.00

Sark Milk Churn, parian with small handle and gilded
  acanthus decorations in relief and bearing in gilded lettering
  Souvenir de Sercq in gilt script. It has no lid   64mm   150.00

Scent Bottle (in Sevres style). Richly gilded with a wide
  turquoise band. This item is 'jewelled' with tiny gilt stones
  set around a central ruby. There is an excellent illustration of
  this item in Marjorie Cawley's *Pictorial Encyclopaedia of
  Goss China*. It may well be unique   approx. 125mm   Unpriced

Large Plate Dia. 345mm

Large Plate Dia. 345mm

Large Winchester College Plate, Dia. 345mm

Oval Platter 'Give us this day Our daily bread'

Oval Platter 'Where Reason Rules The Appetite Obeys'

Oval Plate 'Think, Thank and Thrive'

Early Plate with Glazed Recessed Centre

Unglazed Plate with Vine Pattern in Relief

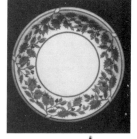

Large Christmas Pudding Plate with Coloured Holly Decoration

Pierced Plate Dia. 300mm

Pierced Comport

Delicate Limpet Shell on Coral Tripod

	£ p

Scent Bottle with decoration in relief of crown over cipher in orange colour   130mm   200.00

Sheep, lying down, identical to those in the **Bullock and Sheep** group. This same sheep re-appeared some half a century later, this time glazed and on an oval plinth as one of the series of animals produced in the 1920s. Glazed or unglazed   115mm   125.00

Shells:
Limpet
An extremely fine glazed limpet shell mounted on a coloured coral tripod base, another example of eggshell porcelain. (Illustrated. Goss Record. 8th Edition: Page 4. Bottom Shelf – front)   66mm   75.00

Nautilus
(a) large glazed and crested version   155mm   75.00
(b) a finer smaller, glazed, uncrested version tinted in pink   95mm   250.00
(Illustrated. Goss Record. 8th Edition: Page 4. Middle Shelf). This is an example of Goss eggshell porcelain

Whelk
(a) a single glazed whelk shell supported on a coral and rock base   144mm   60.00
(b) a group of three glazed whelk shells mounted on a stone base and having coloured coral between the shells   137mm   125.00

Squirrel, standing beside a hollow tree-trunk. Trunk glazed inside for use as a posy vase   117mm   125.00

Tea Service. Odd cups, saucers, plates and jugs, bearing only the impressed W.H. GOSS mark. Cups and saucers are very fine glazed parian ware with raised ivy, vine and grape or other similar pattern. Belleek later used the same design.

Cup and saucer glazed   80mm   60.00

Milk Jug glazed   70mm   50.00

Plate. Round, unglazed   approx. dia. 200mm   50.00

Bread or Cake Plate. Oval, unglazed   Max width 215mm   85.00

Teapot and Lid. Oval   100.00

£   p

Vase, decorated with flying cherubs in relief and two gargoyles
on shoulder. Exhibited at International Exhibition 1862.   293mm   750.00

Vases, Jewelled
These are probably the finest and most beautiful pieces ever
produced by the Goss factory. William H. Goss carried out
hundreds of experiments in order to perfect the parian body,
which the author considers to be among the finest ever
produced. Into this he set stones; some semi-precious, others
glass in the most attractive and decorative way. He patented
the process and was the object of widespread acclaim, for
nobody had yet been able to successfully produce high
quality work of this nature although many, even Sevres, had
tried. Only three examples of jewelled ware are known to
exist and two are illustrated in this Chapter – and one again
in colour on the jacket of *Goss China Arms, Decorations and Their
Values* the sequel to this book by the same author.
(a) **Vase** with oviform body, and pedestal foot, having 597
    jewels coloured green, red, yellow and magenta set
    amongst rich and ornate gilding. Gosshawk mark   155mm   Unpriced
(b) **Vase**, octagonal with two shaped handles. Raised ivy
    leaf pattern, richly gilded with 740 magenta and green
    jewels inset   240mm   Unpriced
(c) **Scent Bottle** See page 206

Vases. A number of early parian vases 70–385mm in height
were produced, each unique. Illustrations of these may be
found in the engraving of W.H. Goss' exhibit for the
International Exhibition of 1862 (see *Goss for Collectors,
The Literature'*, John Magee. Milestone Publications)

Some specific known examples are given here:

Vase. Whorl pattern in relief with lines of alternate blue dots and
gilding   70mm   750.00

Vase. Fluted pattern in relief with three horizontal bands of blue
dots enclosed by gilded lines. Ivy pattern in relief at neck   70mm   750.00

Ewer. Having horizontal blue lines and raised ivy leaf pattern
with two horizontal bands of blue dots enclosed by gilded
bands. One shaped handle to side   70mm   750.00

Vase. having vertical flutes with rich multi-coloured floral
pattern around bulbous centre   100mm   750.00

Vase of Pompeian slender form and having Grecian scenes
in light pastel shades   385mm   750.00

Rare Early Vase

Rare Early Ewer

Rare Early Vase

Rare Jewelled Vase

Rare Jewelled Vase

Three Whelk Shells on Base

Nautilus Shell, large

Rare Vase 293mm

Early Vase, Whorl and Blue Dots Decoration

Angel's Head Wall Vase

Humming Bird Wall Vase

Pompeian Vase, Early with coloured Grecian Scenes

£   p

Wall Vases

(a) Child's Head with radiating hair and feathers, glazed   125mm   155.00
except for the face. Reputedly, the face is that of one of the   150mm   155.00
daughters of W.H. Goss   190mm   200.00

(b) Heads of **Granville, Disraeli, Derby, Georgiana Jewitt
and Bright** in high relief on front of a glazed or unglazed oval
wall-pocket, with plain, blue, or green background and
acanthus leaf surround.

White, unglazed 180mm   150.00

Part-coloured, glazed   250.00

(c) As **(b)** but without head i.e. a wall-vase decorated with
acanthus leaves. Same price.

(d) A Humming Bird, taking nectar from a passion-
flower, and with a nest containing three eggs above in
the surrounding foliage. Glazed   257mm   175.00

Winchester Flagons. These are a pair, unglazed, carrying
coloured likenesses in low relief of:

(a)   The Trusty Servant (if marked W.H. GOSS)   160mm   100.00
(b)   William of Wykeham (if marked W.H. GOSS)   160mm   100.00

Many of these appear unmarked and may possibly have been made by the Goss
factory. One pair, marked, is reputed to exist but has not been seen by the author.
Similar flagons were made by Copeland and other factories for William Savage, the
first Winchester Agent. Unmarked varieties would be worth £20.00–£40.00 depend-
ing on size and desirability.

Goss England and Late Ware

From the latter part of the 1920s, there appeared to be an effort made to bring Goss ware more into line with the wares of contemporary and rival firms. The result was a wide range, varying from figurines to wares which are of poor quality and definitely not the fine parian that the founder developed and used.

While technically the term 'GOSS ENGLAND' dates from the sale of the original firm of W.H. Goss, the 'ENGLAND' was more than occasionally omitted, thereby giving the impression that an item was of somewhat earlier manufacture than it actually was. Give-aways include Coronation wares for Edward the Eighth, and for George VI and Queen Elizabeth, and also for the 1938 Empire Exhibition in Scotland, all of which can be readily found lacking the word 'ENGLAND'.

It would be untrue to say that in the late 1920s no new models were produced by the Goss factory (for we have 'League' Models up to 1932) and it was during this period that the last remaining member of the Goss family to have an interest in the factory, William Huntley Goss, one of the sons of the original W.H. Goss, relinquished his influence. Having invested his all in the firm, success escaped him, and it was only by the sale of the firm to a combine of other 'crested china' manufacturers that liquidation was avoided. The full story of how the W.H. Goss factory fell into other hands will be found in *Crested China* by Sandy Andrews (Milestone Publications 1980).

Most of the items in this section are not 'Goss' proper but the products of other manufacturers appearing with the magic Gosshawk mark for no other reason than that Goss was the market leader, the name that sold goods in hard times. The most common factories were then Arcadian, Willow and Cauldon. The accurate pricing of other crested china has led to a complete re-think of this late period and a complete new list, with totally revised prices, is the result.

A large amount of difficult to describe and list domestic ware of the late period is constantly coming to light. All of this is of relatively little value and the reader is advised to refer to the Domestic and Ornamental Ware Chapter and to take the value of a similar item for the piece in question.

If one has a piece of Cottage Pottery or Royal Buff then that section in this Chapter should be referred to and the value of a similar piece taken.

It should be remembered that all prices in this book are for the *items* of Goss only and *not* for any decorations which may appear on them.

A. Buildings and Monuments

Except where noted, all these models were white-glazed, and
usually carried the appropriate Coat-of-Arms. Many of them
can also be found bearing the manufacturer's mark of an
associated company, usually Willow Art or Arcadian.

		£ p
An Clachan Cottage – in full colour, produced solely as a souvenir of the 1938 Empire Exhibition, at which had been built a full size replica of this Cottage	62mm	650.00
A second version of the **An Clachan Cottage** can also be found – but it is in fact the small version of **Robert Burns' Cottage**, merely re-named and, in the example seen, carrying the motif of the 1938 Exhibition and a GOSS ENGLAND mark	Length 62mm	650.00
Ann Hathaway's Cottage fully coloured	78mm	30.00
	110mm	50.00
	133mm	60.00
Banbury Cross (a) White	127mm	65.00
(b) Brown or Blue/Brown	127mm	170.00
Big Ben	100mm	30.00
	134mm	35.00
	152mm	40.00
	170mm	40.00
Canterbury Cathedral	64mm	55.00
Cenotaph	90mm	17.50
	145mm	30.00
Chesterfield Church	76mm	55.00
Clachan Empire Exhibition Tower and Stadium Glazed, grey, and bearing a late coloured transfer of the 'Clachan Empire Exhibition', 1938 motif. This model may have been intended for use as an ash-tray, as the pictorial portion is 'dished'	125mm	75.00
Clifton Suspension Bridge	64mm	55.00
Edith Cavell Monument	180mm	55.00
Hindhead Sailor's Stone	95mm	40.00
Houses of Parliament	64mm	45.00

Norwich Cathedral

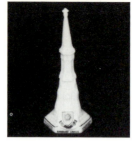

Banbury Cross

Big Ben

Chesterfield Church

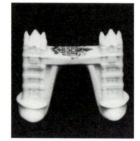

Tower Bridge

St. Paul's Cathedral

The Cenotaph

Westminster Abbey, West Front

Temple Bar

Norwich Edith Cavell Memorial

The Old Curiosity Shop

Windsor Castle, Round Tower

John Knox's House

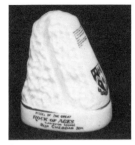

Rock of Ages

Shakespeare's Birthplace

An Clachan Cottage

Shakespeare Bust

Bass Bottle and Glass on Tray

Ashtray, Edward VIII

Box Ashtray, Burns and S.E.E. 1938

Circular Ashtray with Three Rests

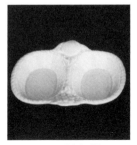

Pottery Jam Dish, Two Section

Shoe, John Waterson's Clog

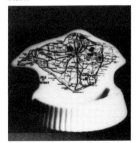

Ashtray with Map of Isle of Wight

		£ p
King Alfred's Statue	170mm	65.00
John Knox's House in full colour	102mm	300.00
Marble Arch, London	57mm	35.00
	40mm	30.00
Nelson's Column	100mm	65.00
Norwich Cathedral	Length 105mm	55.00
Old Curiosity Shop	46mm	55.00
Rock of Ages	79mm	25.00
Rock of Gibraltar, menu holder	Length 160mm	275.00
Rufus Stone	100mm	12.00
Shakespeare's Birthplace in full colour	40mm	30.00
	78mm	30.00
	102mm	50.00
	115mm	55.00
St. Paul's Cathedral	75mm	40.00
	90mm	45.00
	120mm	55.00
Temple Bar	65mm	45.00
Tower Bridge	64mm	55.00
Westminster Abbey	52mm	40.00
	133mm	50.00
Windsor Castle	53mm	50.00
Windsor Round Tower	76mm	35.00
York Minster	56mm	55.00

£   p

B. Flower Girls

These figures were a complete departure from the normal range of Goss wares, and obviously indicated the popularity of the Royal Doulton and Coalport figures which they resemble. Several figures were made in two sizes, and usually measured between 90mm and 170mm in height. The fact that the word 'ENGLAND' may have been omitted from the trade mark should not be taken to indicate a particularly early specimen – they are all late, dating from around 1920–1928.

All but one of these ladies are named, and they are all decorated attractively, most appearing in several different shades.

Annette		135mm	130.00
		100mm	87.50
Balloon Seller		90mm	130.00
		130mm	175.00
Barbara seated on settee		110mm	220.00
Bell Lady		92mm	70.00
Bridesmaid	See page 220	90mm	
		140mm	115.00
Bunty			150.00
Cruet two ladies in full colour, one salt, one pepper, Bridesmaid and Granny		68mm Each	45.00
Daisy		120mm	115.00
Pair of 'Daisy' Flower Girls mounted on Wooden Bookends		Pair	265.00
Doris. Reputed to exist but unverified			
Dutch Girl		140mm	120.00
Edyth		140mm	120.00
Granny		90mm	115.00
Gwenda		130mm	145.00
Joan		130mm	110.00
Lady Beth			155.00

Annette

The Balloon Seller

Barbara

Bell Lady

Bridesmaid, 140mm

Dutch Girl

Cruet Salt

Cruet Pepper

Edyth

Pair of 'Daisy Bookends'
Left-Hand . . .

. . . and Right-Hand

Granny

Gwenda

Lady Betty

Joan

Lady Marie

Lady Rose

Lorna

Miss Julia

Miss Prudence

Mistress Page

Peggy

Phyllis

Un-named Lady, Pink Dress,
Black Bonnet

219

		£ p
Lady Betty	160mm	155.00
Lady Freda		155.00
Lady Marie	145mm	155.00
Lady Rose	170mm	145.00
Lorna	90mm	130.00
Miss Julia	170mm	155.00
Miss Prudence	135mm	155.00
Mistress Ford	100mm	175.00
Mistress Page	105mm	175.00
Peggy	90mm	115.00
	120mm	120.00
Phyllis	95mm	175.00
Un-named Lady Pink dress, black bonnet	170mm	85.00

A series of 6 figures entitled 'The Wedding Group', modelled from the original designs of the American artist C.H. Twelvetrees, were produced as follows:

The Bride 'God Bless Her'	95mm	175.00
The Bridegroom 'God Help Him'	100mm	175.00
The Best Man 'No Wedding Bells for Him'	95mm	220.00
The Mother-in-Law 'But a Very Nice One'	105mm	200.00
The Parson 'Solemn and Businesslike'	100mm	200.00
The Bridesmaid	90mm	95.00

The Bride

The Bridegroom

The Best Man

The Mother-in-Law

The Parson

The Bridesmaid 90mm

Toby Jug 100mm Coloured

Toby Jug 60mm Coloured

Toby Jug 85mm

Toby Jug 90mm Coloured

Toby Jug 100mm Coloured

Churchill Toby Jug

£ p

C. Toby Jugs

Apart from the Stratford Toby Jug and the 'Churchill' Toby Jug, all Goss Toby Jugs are late products and a wide selection of other crested china manufacturers' moulds were used. Sizes range from miniatures, little more than 30mm high, to larger sizes in the region of 200mm high. Female Toby jugs were also made. The same jug is often found in a variety of colours.

British Sailor Toby Jug, blue colouring	60mm	50.00
Toby Jug White glazed and crested	67mm	40.00
	80mm	42.00
Toby Jug Miniature (Male and Female Figures)	40mm	60.00
Toby Jug Multi-coloured (Male and Female Figures)	approx. 70mm	65.00
Toby Jug Multi-coloured, also found with one arm forming a handle	85mm	70.00
	160mm	100.00
	50mm	60.00
Toby Jug Multi-coloured	110mm	85.00
	127mm	40.00
	160mm	100.00

For **Stratford Toby Jug** and **Stratford Toby Basin**
See pages 104 and 106

Churchill Toby Jug with blue or green coat, marked 'copyright 1927' and inscribed on top hat 'Any odds – Bar *one* That's *me* who Kissed the Blarney Stone'	164mm	115.00

£ p

D.   Figures and Animals

Many figures were incorporated into ash-trays, cruets, posy-holders, and other domestic wares – while some appear to be purely ornamental. Ware in this section almost without exception originates from the Arcadian and Willow Art factories. Should you be unable to find a particular piece listed here, please consult *The Price Guide to Crested China* where the model should be found. The price will be similar.

Babies (two) seated on Ash Tray
'That's the one Daddy told Nurse!'   40.00

Black Baby as Ash Tray   60.00

Black Boy – 'Cigarettes'   100mm   60.00

Black Boy and Girl seated on log   80mm   60.00

Black Boys, two seated on log   80mm   60.00

Black Cat in Boot   58mm   45.00

Black Cat on Dish   115mm x 70mm   40.00

Black Cat (seated) on Horse-shoe Shaped Pin Box   70mm   45.00

Black Cat Playing Golf on Golf Ball   60mm   60.00

Black Cat Seated at Head of Horseshoe as Ash Tray Approx. 42mm   45.00

Black Cheshire Cat (identical to white variety)   90mm   65.00

Budgerigar   30.00

Burns, Bust of   136mm   17.50

Caddy, with Bag on Golf Ball   60.00

Cat, Seated   30.00

Cat, Seated, with White or Coloured Bow at Neck   60mm   30.00

Cheshire Cat (No base), white or coloured   98mm   30.00

Chicken White or coloured   50mm   30.00

Crest Faced Man with Coat-of-Arms on flat face   80mm   35.00

Cat, Seated with Bow

Cat, Seated

Budgerigar

Dog, with One Ear Up

Dog, Squat, One Ear Up

Scottie Dog, Length 260mm

Chicken

Rabbit

Rhinoceros

Plaice

Shetland Pony

Duck Posy Holder

Punch and Judy Pepper and Salt

Pixie on a Toadstool

White Boy Holding Open Matchbox

English Folksong Bride

Falstaff

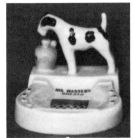

Dog and Whiskey Bottle on Ash Tray

Two Coloured Children on Log

Black Cat in Boot

Black Cat on Horseshoe Tray

Two Babies on Tray

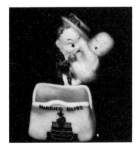

Father and Child Beside Open Bag 'Married Bliss'

Gin and It

			£ p
Cruet. Punch (Salt), Judy (Pepper) and Toby (Mustard) in full colour – all on tray			85.00
NOTE: Items from the above set may be found white glazed or in varying shades of lustre		Price each	17.50
Dog and Whisky Bottle on Ash Tray 'His Master's Breath'			40.00
Dog, Scottie with blue Tam O'Shanter		60mm	30.00
Dog, Scottie, Black and White with glass eyes		Length 260mm	120.00
Dog, squat, one ear up, some colouring			30.00
Dog, with one ear up. White or Coloured		90mm	30.00
English Folksong Bride standing beside ancient chest		93mm	55.00
Falstaff	(a) Coloured	150mm	85.00
	(b) White	150mm	60.00
Fish, Plaice Two sizes		One, Length 125mm	25.00
Frog		60mm	30.00
'Gin and It' Two seated ladies at side of dish, coloured.		100mm x 65mm	40.00
Golfer, standing on golf-ball, holding clubs – in centre of hexagonal dish		90mm x 75mm	45.00
Gnome, standing carrying a shell under each arm. Fully coloured			200.00
Jester on Ashtray, coloured		64mm	40.00
(Ann) Hathaway Bust		80mm	15.00
		135mm	22.00
Hippopotamus		Length 88mm	60.00
Lady in Bathing Costume and Cap on Ash Tray			40.00
Lady Godiva on Horseback. Small, glazed		80mm	40.00
Lady Reclining on Top of Box coloured		100mm x 85mm	200.00
Lifeboat Man		140mm	27.50
'Married Bliss' Posy Vase (Coloured)			
(a) Girl, holding baby, with open bag in front			40.00
(b) Man, holding baby, with open bag in front			40.00

		£ p
New Forest Pony	65mm	35.00
Norwich Canary	94mm	100.00
Nude Female Seated on rock. Coloured (For flower arrangement)	190mm	60.00
Penguin	90mm	35.00
Penguin on Ash Tray	92mm	40.00
Pig, with verse	80mm	35.00
Pixie. Seated on toadstool. (Coloured)	54mm	50.00
Policeman, with raised hand: 'Stop'	94mm	40.00
Rabbits, blue, yellow, green, brown or Royal Buff	40mm	15.00
	50mm	15.00
	60mm	15.00
	80mm	20.00
	100mm	25.00
Rabbit, White	60mm	15.00
Race-horse and Jockey. Oval base, some colouring	108mm	200.00
Royston Crow	94mm	175.00
Scots Boy on Dish	90mm	40.00
Scottish Lion. Stylized, standing on square ashtray base. Scottish Empire Exhibition 1938. Coloured, green trim	103mm	50.00

Shakespeare Bust	(a)	White, unglazed	80mm	15.00
	(b)	White, unglazed	110mm	20.00
	(c)	White, unglazed	135mm	22.00
	(d)	Bronzed	135mm	30.00

		£ p
Shell	70mm	15.00
Shetland Pony No base	76mm	35.00
Swan	50mm	25.00
Trusty Servant. Coloured. Not to be confused with the earlier variety	132mm	110.00
Toucan. Coloured, on an Ash Tray shaped like the bird's foot	61mm	45.00
Welsh Lady. Bust. With some colouring	62mm	30.00
White Boy holding open matchbox as holder 'Matches'	100mm	30.00

227

£   p

E. Late Ware carrying the 'W.H. Goss and Gosshawk' and 'W.H. Goss England' trade marks

Ash Tray. Circular with three rests	Dia. 70mm	10.00
Ash Tray. Round, with raised back in shape of Isle of Wight and bearing coloured map of same	70mm	45.00
Ash Tray. Oval, with rests at each end	Length 100mm	10.00
Ash Tray. Square, card symbols in each corner	60mm sq.	17.50
Ash Tray. Box-shaped. Thistle, spray of heather, Burns transfer, Burns' cottage transfer and Scottish Empire Exhibition motif appear on this and similar very late pieces	Length 120mm	20.00
Ash Tray Various colours – 'Edward VIII, Crowned May 12 1937' in low relief	Dia. 132mm	22.50
Basket. Biscuit colour, with tiny flowers at base of handle	90mm x 75mm	35.00
Basket containing six milk bottles	50mm	25.00
Bass Bottle and Glass on Dish	60mm x 35mm	30.00
Bass Bottle and Silver Beer Mug on Dish	115mm x 70mm	30.00
Bon-Bon Dish. Basket weave design or plain with brown handles	157mm	15.00
Boot	70mm x 40mm	20.00
Bottle with Cork	60mm x 70mm	22.50
Bottle 'One Special Irish' or **'One Special Scotch'** with cork	95mm	25.00
Bucket	55mm	15.00
Cake Plate. Burns, thistles, heather and S.E.E. 1938 decoration	Width 250mm	25.00
Chamber Pot	55mm x 40mm	15.00
Cheese, Dish, green	Length 165mm	12.00

Mug with Little Red Riding Hood Scene

Bulbous Milk Jug

Octagonal Sugar Bowl, Late

Honey Section Dish and Cover with Bee Knob

Welsh Lady Teapot

Beehive preserve Pot ana Cover

Bowl, shown here with 1938 S.E.E. Motif

Cream Jug, Double Lip, No Handle

Green Posy Ring

Mug 80mm

Cottage Pottery Plate 'Shakespearian Cottages'

Cake Plate Burns and S.E.E. 1938

229

		£ p
Chess Pawn	50mm	25.00
Chess Rook	50mm	20.00
Coronation Mug 1937 – King George VI and Queen Elizabeth. This and any other item bearing this design would be worth approximately	80mm	25.00
Cruet Salt Castor in form of an apple, coloured	30mm	25.00
Pepper Castor in form of an orange, coloured	30mm	25.00
Basket, coloured beige to hold the above	Length 80mm	15.00
Cream Jug, double lip, no handle		4.00
Dish. Oval, with tapered sides, green trim, and rose decoration inside		20.00
Egg, with Flapper's Head	38mm	20.00
Fireplace with Kettle and Black Cat – 'There's No Place Like Home' or 'Home Sweet Home'	90mm x 90mm	30.00
Fruit Bowl, orange lustre	Height 110mm Dia. 245mm	15.00
Lantern. Coloured, hexagonal, with handle	200mm	75.00
Mug with floral decoration, two handled	133mm	17.50
Mug, one-handled	100mm	10.00
Mug, Little Red Riding Hood Scene	100mm	60.00
Open Umbrella	50mm x 35mm	20.00
Orange-shaped and coloured marmalade jar	88mm	40.00
Posy Dish. Blue or green. Circular	Dia. 155mm	8.50
Prime Cheddar Cheese		22.50
Puzzle Jug	70mm	22.50
Rose Bowl. Pink, with green foliage	80mm x 50mm	20.00
Salt and Pepper Pots Bulbous, usually found with late transfer decoration	Pair 54mm	17.50
Shaving Mug	100mm	40.00

		£ p
Shoe (John Waterson's Clog in Arcadian)	Length 80mm	30.00
Slipper	38mm	27.50
Sugar Basin, octagonal	Dia. 70mm	4.00
Sweetmeat Dish, green	Length 165mm	12.00
Thimble	38mm	30.00
Toast-Rack, green	Length 100mm	12.00
Tea-pot in form of Welsh Lady, coloured	152mm	60.00
Vases. Various shapes and sizes under 70mm	Each around	3.00
Weston-Super-Mare Floral Clock Surround coloured		60.00
Whisky Bottle, Soda Syphon and Glass on		
(a) Horse-shoe Ash Tray	87mm	30.00
(b) Thistle Ash Tray	87mm	30.00
Whisky Bottle. Hip-flask type – 2 piece	120mm	40.00

MARGARET GOSS DECORATIONS: Normally identifiable by the monogrammed letters 'M.G.' and the date 1922. Margaret Goss was a grand-daughter of William Henry Goss and daughter of William Huntley Goss. Margaret (known as Peggy) designed a number of coloured scenes, usually depicting humourous animal and nursery rhyme themes for childrens' mugs and plates. See *Goss China Arms, Decorations and Their Values*, p. 100 for a full list and additional value.

COLOURED AND LUSTRE ITEMS
Items such as coffee and tea cups and saucers, sugar bowls milk jugs, teaplates, pin trays, candle holders etc. appear in a variety of colours and lustres. Details of these are given in *Goss China Arms, Decorations and Their Values*. Prices of items so decorated range from £7.00–£15.00 and a teapot or larger item in the region of £20.00.

F. Ware marked 'W.H. Goss Cottage Pottery' or 'Royal Buff'

COTTAGE TEA SERVICE

All pieces are in the shape of a coloured cottage
  excepting cups, saucers and plates.

		£ p
Biscuit Barrel	150mm	25.00
Butter Dish and Lid	Length 107mm	17.50
Cakeplate	Dia. 240mm	17.50
Cheese Dish and Cover	Length 170mm	25.00
Cottage Mustard Pot	50mm	16.50
Cottage Pepper Shaker	50mm	16.50
Cottage Salt Shaker	50mm	16.50
Cup and Saucer	75mm	15.00
Milk Jug	60mm	13.00
	108mm	15.00
Sugar Basin and Lid	110mm	15.00
Sugar Bowl	60mm	13.00
Teaplate	Dia. 150mm	13.00
Teapot	115mm	30.00
Toast Rack (a) To hold four slices	Length 100mm	26.50
(b) To hold two slices	Length 70mm	22.50

COTTAGE POTTERY

Beaker taper, one handle	85mm	10.00
	114mm	13.00
Butter Dish in wooden surround 'Take a little butter'. Decorated with tulips or similar	Dia. 115mm	10.00
Coffee Pot, octagonal	200mm	25.00
Cup and Saucer, octagonal	65mm	13.00

		£ p
Cup and Saucer	75mm	13.00
Duck. Coloured posy holder. Bears inscription on base: 'Hand-painted under glazed porcelain by GOSS'	Length 100mm Height 58mm	45.00
Four Egg Cups on Stand, Basket Weave	Set	30.00
Six Egg Cups on Stand. Basket Weave	Set	40.00
Honey Pot and Lid. Beehive shaped with bee as knob on lid	80mm	20.00
Horeshoe decorative. Appears in several pastel shades	120mm	15.00
Jam Dish Two section basket weave	Length 170mm	10.00
Jug, cylindrical or bulbous	85mm	12.30
'Little Brown Jug' Several sizes all carrying title or verse and some also a Black Cat transfer	60mm – 180mm	15.00
Milk Jug	70mm	13.00
Mug. Two-handled, decorated with apples, and carrying the quotation 'Yaas, 'tis thirsty work – 'ave a drop o' Zomerzet Zider'.	102mm	30.00
Pepper Castor, shaped	90mm	10.00
Plate. Coloured, depicting Shakesperian cottages	Dia. 220mm	22.00
Plate. With inscription 'Education is Better than Wealth'	265mm x 230mm	30.00
Preserve Pot and Lid. Poppies and 'East, West, Home is Best' or similar decoration and verse	110mm	18.50
Salt Castor, shaped	90mm	10.00
Sugar Basin	60mm	13.00
Tankard, Widdicombe Fair decoration	125mm	35.00
Tankard, shaped, one handle	95mm	12.00

Cottage Pottery Two-handled Mug 102mm

Shaped Vase

Late Floral Decoration Inset into Lip-salve Pot Base, Lustre

Coloured Lantern

Weston-Super-Mare Floral Clock-holder

2 slice Toastrack and Preserve Dish

Cottage Pottery Cup and Saucer

Cottage Pottery Preserve Pot and Lid

The Little Brown Jug

Cottage Pottery Pepper Pot

Cottage Pottery Cheese Dish

Cottage Pottery Four Slice Toast Rack

		£	p
Teapot, Taper	115mm	25.00

Toastrack and Two section Marmalade Dish		
Basket Weave	Length 175mm	16.50

| **Toastrack** with coloured Pixie seated at each end | 80mm | 35.00 |

G. 'Hand Painted' Ware

Beside the normal 'W.H. GOSS ENGLAND' trade mark, there is also a 'Handpainted' mark which is usually found on domestic ware, 'Royal Buff' and 'Cottage Pottery' which cover a large range of items, varying from a cottage-shaped tea set to a pottery (as opposed to porcelain) range of 'Little Brown Jugs', beakers, cups and saucers and various other items of domestic ware. See Section F.

Obviously the original Goss moulds were still available at this period, and a number were used to carry a range of floral patterns ranging from delicate pastel shades to rather garish hand-painted examples.

It is difficult to accurately list all late ware as there are so many variations. If you have a similar piece to one shown then a price in the same region will apply. The reader should consult also the Chapter on 'Domestic and Ornamental Wares' and 'Parian' after checking all the possibilities in 'Goss England'.

See *Goss China: Arms, Decorations and their Values* for full details and values of all decorations on Goss china.

Miniatures

A range of fine miniature items was produced in eggshell porcelain. The plates in particular are extremely fine.

KEY TO DECORATIONS

A   Forget-Me-Nots
B   Blackpool or other Coats-of-Arms
C   No decoration (except blue and gold dots on Jugs only)
D   Shamrock, Horse-shoe and 'GOOD LUCK'
E   Trusty Servant
F   Thistles
G   Shamrocks

Miniature Tea Service on oval tray
Comprising Oval Crinkle Tray, 165mm long, four cups and saucers, teapot with lid, sugar bowl and milk jug. Four Dia. 38mm plates can also be found but are as rare as the 60mm cake plate.

Miniature Tea Service on square tray
Comprising 70mm square tray, cup and saucer, tea pot with lid, sugar bowl and milk jug.

Prices for each piece:

Decoration	Teapot and Lid 35mm	Cup and Saucer 16mm	Milk Jug 20mm	Sugar Basin Dia. 28mm	Tea Plate Dia. 38mm	Cake Plate Dia. 60mm	Square Tray Width 70mm	Oval Tray Length 165mm	Addition for Complete Set
A	35.00	26.00	22.00	22.00	35.00	45.00	20.00	25.00	25.00
B									
C		20.00		17.50	30.00				
D									
E	45.00	30.00	27.50	27.50	45.00		25.00	35.00	25.00
F	45.00	30.00	27.50	27.50			25.00	35.00	30.00
G	45.00	30.00	27.50	27.50			20.00	35.00	25.00

*Miniature Tea Service on
Oval Tray, forget-me-nots*

Oval Tray, forget-me-nots

*Miniature Beaker, Trusty
Servant*

*Miniature Tea Service on
Square Tray, Trusty Servant*

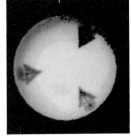

*Miniature Teaplate,
forget-me-nots*

*Miniature Vase Two
Handles, Shamrock,
Horseshoe and Good Luck*

Miniature Jug, Thistles

Miniature Bowl, plain

*Cup and Saucer
forget-me-nots*

*Milk Jug and Sugar
Basin forget-me-nots*

*Jug and Bowl
Blue and Gold dots*

*Teapot and lid,
Trusty Servant*

Jug and Bowl Set

Height of Jug 20mm Diameter of Bowl 35mm   All sizes are the same price.
         25mm   40mm
         30mm   45mm

Each item priced separately. No premium is to be added for a matched set. The 20mm Jug doubles as the milk jug in tea services.

Decoration	Jug or Bowl
	£ p
A	15.00
B	7.00
C	15.00
D	15.00
E	22.00
F	22.00
G	15.00

Vase, Two-handled   20mm   All same price regardless of size
                       25mm
                       30mm

	£ p
A	20.00
B	20.00
C	20.00
D	25.00
E	30.00
F	30.00
G	25.00

Miniature Beaker   19mm

E	£40.00

Bottle and Four-beaker set on 70mm square tray

E	£250.00

A miniature is not known to have a particular decoration where no letter or price is given

Terra-Cotta

Terra-cotta wares are reasonably scarce products of the Goss factory and date from the short period of Goss' partnership with Mr. Peake, a roofing tile manufacturer, in 1867.

Wares are usually marked 'W.H. GOSS' in black printed capitals but items marked 'GOSS & PEAKE' are particularly desirable, and also represent an unusual departure from the normal range of Goss products.

These wares are difficult to categorize accurately. They are usually decorated with black and coloured designs, classical figures or cartoons.

			£ p
Busts (a) **Robert Burns,** socle base		165mm	300.00
(b) **George Dawson,** dated 1871		305mm	500.00
(c) **Charles Swain**		280mm	500.00
Candle Holders			65.00
Comports			75.00
Jardinieres usually found with base plates – often unmarked			65.00
Jugs, including the 'Cambridge Jug' which is sometimes found with a pewter hinged lid. Often found un-named			50.00–75.00
Spill Holders			65.00
Tea Pots			80.00
Tobacco Jars. These are relatively common		130mm–150mm	50.00
A Richly Decorated Winged Vase illustrated in colour in Marjory Cawley's *Pictorial Encyclopaedia of Goss China*		516mm	800.00
A Black-enamelled Terra-cotta Vase having Classical Figures stencilled around the body.		180mm	200.00
Vases of Varying Heights and Shapes			50.00–100.00
Bag Vase with pictorial view of The Cassino, Barbados Aquatic Club, and Arms of Barbados on the reverse.		50mm	75.00

Terra-cotta Bust of Burns

Terra-cotta Tobacco Jar, Patterned

Terra-cotta Tobacco Jar, Cartoons

Terra-cotta Tobacco Jar, Cartoons

Terra-cotta Spill Holder, Patterned

Terra-cotta Spill Holder, Cartoons

Terra-cotta comport, Patterned

Terra-cotta Vase, Patterned

Terra-Cotta Vase and Stopper, Cartoons

Black Enamelled Terra-cotta Vase

Terra-cotta Bag-Vase, Barbados Transfer

Terra-cotta Keystone, Lord Beaconsfield

240

£   p

'The Keystones of the Kingdom'
being virtually life-size heads of
(a) Lord Derby
(b) Lord Beaconsfield
mounted on 'Keystone' shaped slabs (dated 1876)
One example also has impressed on rear in addition to the
W.H. Goss mark 'WETLEY BRICK AND
POTTERY CO. LIMITED. W.K.' One wonders
whether they were all made by this firm.
Height 321mm; Width 195mm reducing to 150mm   each   350.00
NOTE: See also Parian A for an unglazed
white variety.

Advertising Ware

An unusual Oval Plaque distributed to Goss Agents in the later
period, i.e. after 1927. Stating 'AGENT FOR W.H. GOSS
ART – POTTERY' in red between two Gosshawks   Length 220mm   250.00

The Plaque from a Goss Cabinet.   70mm   75.00
   The shield shape carrying the Goss family arms

A Goss Agent's Change Tray
One was given to each Agent and bore the arms of his
   particular town.   Dia. 140mm   150.00
Examples without arms may also be found

Plaque shaped to form Ann Hathaway's Cottage,
   coloured   50.00

Plaque featuring a toby jug in colour.   50.00

Goss Agent's enamel shop-front sign.
   Shield shaped   Height   300mm   125.00

Dolls

Porcelain heads for dolls were normally imported from the Continent, but during, and particularly towards the end of the First World War, supplies from that source disappeared. For a short period, probably about a year, the Goss factory produced a series of dolls' heads. Whether or not arms and hands were also produced has never been determined, and it was normal practice for the heads to be passed to another firm to have a body, limbs, and, if necessary, hair, added. The body was normally made of stuffed flesh-coloured cotton material, and carried a purple stamp on it, which has not yet been deciphered.

Arms have been made in porcelain, and also in a somewhat softer composition (papier mache?) but feet have rarely been other than a cloth extension of the legs. Sometimes arms and legs have been jointed, but on smaller specimens have been one piece.

Finished dolls vary considerably in height, and examples have been found as short as 350mm and as tall as 650mm.

With regard to the actual Goss heads, these come in a variety of sizes and patterns. Painted eyes are perhaps more common, but glass eyes were also used. Where hair has been applied, this has normally been found to be mohair, but this would have been added by the body manufacturer. 'Character' dolls were also made, with hair moulded onto the head.

Identification of Goss dolls is by the simple word 'Goss' impressed into the back of the porcelain, and it is unlike any other Goss impressed mark.

Ideally, Goss dolls should be dressed in clothes made at the time, but much renovation and restoration, even to the extent of fitting new bodies, has taken place over the years.

Value is dependent on size, body condition, originality of the clothing – and prices will reflect this.

Price range £200.00 – £350.00

No. 1 Fountains Abbey Cup

No. 2 Aberdeen Bronze Pot

No. 3 Ancient Welsh Crochon

No. 4 York Roman Ewer

No. 5 Loving Cup

No. 6 Chester Roman Vase

No. 7 Bath Bronze Ewer

No. 8 Irish Mather

Late Goss Agents Sign

Goss Doll

Goss Doll

Goss Agents Change Tray

Postcards

'Goss' postcards were published with the permission of W.H. Goss by S.A. Oates & Co. of Halifax who printed on them: "None genuine without the name 'Goss' ".

These cards were published in the latter half of the Edwardian Era, postmarks ranging from 1905 to 1912.

They carry the word 'Goss' in gold on a dark blue circular motif in the top left-hand corner, and the description of the particular model at the base. (Similarly in gold and on a blue background.) The cards are basically photographs of selected models without coats-of-arms. It was then for the local agent or stationer to order cards with their own particular town's coat-of-arms on them. These arms were then over-printed, a process which gives certain combinations of arms and models a peculiar 'flat/round' appearance.

Originally, six cards were produced and sold, if required, in sets, in special envelopes. Later, two further cards were added to the range, and it is these two which are the rarities. The cards are numbered in gold in the top right-hand corner, and are as follows:

Card No.	Model	Price
		£ p
1	Abbot's Cup, Fountains Abbey	3.50
2	Aberdeen Bronze Pot	3.50
3	Ancient Welsh Bronze Crochon	3.50
4	Roman Ewer from York	3.50
5	Loving Cup	3.50
6	Roman Vase from Chester	3.50
7	Bronze Ewer from Bath	8.50
8	Irish Mather	8.50

Prices quoted are for cards in good condition.

Goss Cabinets

These were introduced by J. J. Jarvis, editor of *The Goss Record* and were available from 1905 until 1919.

They were manufactured in six basic types by the firm who made the bookcases for the Encyclopaedia Britannica Company. The following details are taken from the Seventh Edition of the *Goss Record*:–

These cabinets have been specially designed to hold Collections of Heraldic Porcelain, although equally suitable for other varieties of China, Bric-a-brac, etc. Made by one of the leading wholesale Cabinet Makers in the country to the personal instructions of the compiler of the GOSS RECORD, no expense has been spared to produce the most suitable Cabinets to display to advantage the varied shapes of Goss Porcelain obtainable, and the Arms emblazoned thereon.

Every Cabinet is substantially made and well finished. The shelves are lined with green cloth, and the doors fitted with lock and key. They may be had in either Chippendale or Fumed Oak as stated, whilst some are made in both, and each style is priced at the lowest possible figure consistent with the finest workmanship.

A fully illustrated list of Cabinets will be sent on application to the Goss Record Office.

The Cabinets will be sent from the makers direct on receipt of remittance, the carriage being paid by purchasers on delivery; 5s. will be charged for cases and packing unless these are returned carriage paid within 7 days.

The amount paid will be returned in full for any Cabinet not approved of and returned carriage paid upon receipt.

Cabinets may be obtained on the "Times" system of monthly instalments, particulars of which may be had on application.

All Cabinets bear the "Goss Arms" on a specially designed porcelain shield, without which none are genuine.

There are seven types of Cabinets as under: Current Value
£ p

Design A. A small revolving cabinet in Chippendale to stand on a pedestal or table. 18-ins. square. Holding capacity, 50 average sized pieces inside and 25 outside. Step-shaped shelves from the bottom. Glass sides and top. **Price £2 2 0** 250.00

Design B. Wall Cabinet 3-ft. 3-ins. wide by 3-ft. 8-ins. high. Holding capacity, 85 pieces. Made in Fumed Oak. A very artistic and pleasing case. **Price £2 18 6** 300.00

Design BB. The same as B, but with an additional shelf. This will hold 100 pieces. **Price £3 3 0** 300.00

Design C. A revolving case in Chippendale, somewhat similar to A, but 3-ft. 4-ins. high and 1-ft. 5-ins. wide. This will hold 120 pieces, and where space is a consideration, is an excellent Cabinet. **Price £3 7 6** 300.00

Design D. As illustration. 4-ft. 6-ins. long by 3-ft. high. Made both in Chippendale and Fumed Oak. The centre door is hinged at the bottom enabling the entire contents to be displayed at once. By a unique mechanical contrivance this door is quite firm when opened. Holding capacity, 125 pieces. **Price £4 4 0** 400.00

Design E. A handsome Cabinet on legs to stand on the ground, and sliding doors 3-ft. wide and 4-ft high, will hold 160 pieces. Made in Chippendale or Fumed Oak. **Price £5 5 0** 400.00

Design F. 5-ft. 2-ins. high by 4-ft. wide. Also made in both woods. A very fine Cabinet to hold nearly 200 pieces. The centre is recessed and enclosed by two doors below and one folding door above (as Cabinet D.), whilst the sides are glazed as well as the front. **Price £7 7 0** 600.00

See Goss Record. 8th Edition: Page 109 for illustration of cabinet D in fumed oak.

The porcelain shield alone is priced at £75.00 and this is included in the values given above.

Cabinets A and C were of the revolving variety, Cabinets B and D were for attaching to the wall, whilst E and F were free-standing.

The Goss Records

In 1900, a keen Goss enthusiast, Mr J.J. Jarvis of Enfield, Middlesex saw the need for a list of Goss agents throughout the country. He wrote to William Henry Goss who, in reply, said that he could not see the need for such a list and would not assist in its publication. Not to be deterred, Jarvis produced a duplicated list which sold out rapidly, as did a Second Edition.

Spurred on by collectors, Jarvis then wrote to every agent seeking accurate information for a properly printed record which appeared, 20 pages in length, in 1901. In April 1902 an eight page supplement, the Second Edition, was published and this updated the previous edition.

In 1903 the Third Edition appeared, 36 pages in length, and now contained lists of models, advertisements and much additional information. The Fourth Edition was a supplement to the Third.

In 1905 however, the Fifth Edition appeared, now 68 pages long and with very much larger lists of both models and agents, thus showing the rapid rise in the variety and output of the Goss factory since 1900. The League of Goss Collectors was announced for the first time, as were Goss Cabinets. The Sixth Edition appeared in 1906 and carried the news of the death of William Henry in January of that year. Now 96 pages in length, it was by this time a veritable mine of information.

Three years elapsed before the 72 page Seventh Edition appeared in October 1909. Jarvis announced that a total of 70,000 of the various editions had been sold to date and that the Eighth Edition would be published in 1912. In fact it appeared in 1914, before the start of the First World War, and Jarvis had by that time handed publication over to Evans Bros, the London publishers, who produced a 104 page book. It may be said that Goss collecting reached its peak in this year, and that this edition was the best of them all. It has recently been reprinted by Milestone Publications and provides a fascinating insight into the early days of the hobby.

The Great War took both the firm's customers and employees for war service and when the War Edition was published in 1916, it was a 24 page supplement to the Eighth Edition, due only to a shortage of paper. This has also been reprinted by Milestone and details will be found on page 251.

The final edition to appear was the Ninth in 1919. 80 pages in length it announced that Goss Cabinets were no longer available. Jarvis had probably died by this time as there are very few introductionary notes for the collector, and those that appear are not in his friendly style.

Goss collecting was by now in decline and ten years later production from the Goss factory ceased.

A list of every edition with present values follows:

Goss Record	*Value*
	£ p
1st Edition	50.00
2nd Edition (Supplement to 1st)	50.00
3rd Edition	50.00
4th Edition (Supplement to 3rd)	50.00
5th Edition	25.00
6th Edition	20.00
7th Edition	20.00
8th Edition	15.00
War Edition (Supplement to 8th)	20.00
9th Edition	15.00

The Goss Records served a two-fold purpose, quite apart from being an advertising medium. Firstly, they gave as full a list as was known at the time of the Goss Models and other wares then available, and secondly, they listed all known agents for the sale of Goss china.

It must be appreciated that Mr Jarvis was not an employee of the Goss firm, and, therefore, that his model lists were incomplete, lacking both the earlier discontinued items and also, of course, all items subsequently produced.

The First Edition of *The Goss Record* listed some 136 models, and the Ninth Edition in 1921 some 400, these figures indicating the rise of the firm during that period. The lists of agents are some 60–70 years out of date but it is good fun to look them up and see what stands at the address today. You never know!

The League of Goss Collectors

The League of Goss Collectors was formed in 1905. The initial subscription was 2/6d which entitled the member to a certificate of membership, a copy of the *Goss Record* as and when published and a special piece of porcelain bearing the Goss Arms. These Goss Arms were surrounded by the wording 'The League of Goss Collectors', and each model, except the first-issued, bore beneath it the statement 'This model is issued to Members of the League and cannot be bought'.

Towards the end of the 1914–18 War, the League spread its wings to become 'The International League of Goss Collectors', and a new model was issued for each year until 1932. These models, together with re-issues of all but the first model, bore a new motif, indicative of the 'International' aspect of the League.

These are the League Models issued:

On joining the League	The Portland Vase.
For members of two years' standing	Ancient Costril or Pilgrim's Bottle.
For members of four years' standing	Staffordshire Tyg.
For members of six years' standing	King's Newton Anglo-Saxon Cinerary Urn.

1918	Cirencester Roman Ewer.
1919	Contact Mine.
1920	Gnossus Vase.
1921	Greek Amphora Vase.
1922	Italian Krater.
1923	Egyptian Lotus Vase.
1924	Wilderspool Roman Tetinae or Feeding Bottle.
1925	Cyprus Mycenaean Vase.
1926	Staffordshire Drinking Cup.
1927	Colchester Roman Lamp.
1928	Fimber Cinerary Urn.
1929	Irish Cruisken.
1930	Northwich Sepulchral Urn.
1931	Chester Roman Altar.
1932	Cheshire Roman Urn.

These pieces are listed and valued in the 'Named Models and Special Shapes' chapter.

Other titles available from
Milestone Publications

Please send for full catalogue

Crested China. The History of Heraldic Souvenir Ware
Sandy Andrews

The 1984 Price Guide to Crested China including revisions to
Crested China
Nicholas Pine and Sandy Andrews

Goss China: Arms, Decorations and their values (1982)
Nicholas Pine

Take Me Back To Dear Old Blighty.
The Great War through the eyes of the Heraldic China Manufacturers
Robert Southall

Arcadian Arms China Catalogue (reprinted)

The Goss Record 8th Edition (1914) (reprinted)

The Goss Record War Edition (1916) (reprinted)

Goss for Collectors – The Literature
John Magee

Let's Collect Goss China
Alf Hedges

A Handbook of Goss China
John Galpin

W.H. Goss and Goss Heraldic China
Norman Emery F.L.A.

Heraldic China Mementoes of the First World War
Surg. Capt. P.D. Gordon-Pugh

Goss & Crested China. Illustrated monthly catalogues
Available by Annual Subscription. Details upon request

CRESTED CHINA
By Sandy Andrews

This title, first published in 1980, fills a large gap in knowledge on the subject, being the first serious and comprehensive reference work ever attempted – although written in a readable light-hearted style.

A large, lavish production with hard cover and colour dust jacket, it contains 304 pages. Over 750 illustrations – 90 in full colour – are included, depicting over 1000 pieces from all factories and showing items from every possible theme with special emphasis on animals, buildings and Great War crested china.

Particulars of well over 4000 pieces are given with their dimensions and relevant details where thought to be of interest. This is the first attempt at a complete listing of all the pieces made by every factory. The history of and all known information about over 220 factories is provided, and a mass of other exciting facts answer all the questions that collectors have been asking for years such as 'Why does the same piece appear with a different factory mark?' 'Why do some pieces have no crest, factory mark or name?' 'Why are some pieces numbered?'; etc. etc.

In addition to all this information, over 270 line drawings of factory marks are shown to aid identification, the majority of which are not in any of the usual 'mark books'.

The story of crested china, how the trade expanded, and some of the colourful characters involved in it is told for the first time. A chapter on the W.H. Goss factory with illustrations of pieces from all periods of that factory's life, throws important new light on the later period and what happened during the Goss England era about which there is often confusion.

The book is not a price guide, although indications of rare items are given, but a lasting, profusely illustrated reference work which is recommended to all crested china enthusiasts.

303mm × 220mm. 304 pages. Cased. 753 illustrations. £14.95

Available from bookshops everywhere or by post direct from Milestone Publicataions. Descriptive leaflets on this and all other titles connected with Goss and crested china sent on request.

The 1984 Price Guide to Crested China
has been designed and produced as a companion to **Crested China**

Goss China Arms, Decorations and their Values
Nicholas Pine

Goss China collecting was a craze during late Victorian and Edwardian times. Tens of thousands of pieces of Goss Heraldic Porcelain were sold throughout the country as souvenirs to bring home for the family what-not or mantlepiece. This fascinating book, written by the leading authority on the subject, lists, describes and values all the different coats-of-arms and decorations which appear on Goss models – over 7000 of them.

A fully revised and updated version of the original book, first published in 1978, this new edition includes over 400 new additions and countless detail improvements, amendments and corrections, making it a truly definitive listing of virtually every known decoration.

In addition, up-to-date market values are given throughout the book showing the premium to be added to a piece for a crest or decoration.

Its 13 chapters include: U.K. and overseas arms, Royal, Nobility, Educational, Ecclesiastical, Commemorative, Transfer printed, Regimental, Flora & Fauna, Flags, Welsh, Masonic and late decorations. These are further sub-divided into 55 easy-to-use sections – **With prices**.

The book contains 415 illustrations in 120 packed pages and is sewn and strongly case bound with a full colour jacket.

The book has been designed for use in conjunction with **The Price Guide to Goss China** by the same author. Collectors and dealers who possess a copy of the price guide are strongly advised to acquire the new book so that accurate up-to-date values may be obtained for each piece, for, as often as not, the decoration on a particular piece is worth much more than the piece itself.

245mm × 213mm. 120 pages. 415 illustrations. £9.95.

Goss & Crested China Ltd. are the leading dealers in Heraldic China

We have been buying and selling for over fifteen years and our experienced staff led by Nicholas Pine will be able to answer your questions and assist you whether you are a novice or an experienced collector.

We have a constantly changing attractively priced stock of some 5000 pieces at our Horndean showrooms including Goss cottages, fonts, crosses, shoes, lighthouses, models etc. and the full range of crested ware including military, animals, buildings etc. covering all the other manufacturers.

Visitors are welcome to call during business hours of 9.00–5.30 any day except Sunday. Those travelling long distances are advised to telephone for an appointment so that they may be sure to receive personal attention upon arrival.

Most of our business is by mail order and we publish 'Goss & Crested China', a monthly 24–28 page illustrated catalogue containing hundreds of pieces for sale from every theme and in every price range. The catalogue is available by annual subscription; please send for details.

In addition, if you specialise, we will be pleased to offer you particular pieces or crests from time to time as suitable items become available. Please let us know your wants as with our ever changing stock we will probably have something to suit.

Our service is personal and friendly and all orders and correspondence are dealt with by return. You will find us fair and straightforward to deal with, as we really care about crested china and we hope that this is reflected in our service.

Finally, we are just as keen to buy as we are to sell and offers of individual items or whole collections are always welcome. These will be dealt with by return and the very highest offers will be made.

Milestone Publications
Goss & Crested China Ltd.
62 Murray Road,
Horndean,
Hampshire
PO8 9JL.
Telephone: Horndean (0705) 597440

SB